AN ANALYSIS OF THE BODO SHORT STORIES

KRITIKAMAL SWARGIARY

Made with ♥ on the Notion Press Platform
www.notionpress.com

Contents

CHAPTER ONE

Some New Reflection in Bodo Short Stories

Abstract

Short stories are one of the essential components of modern literature. It is one of the mind attracting means in the world of Literature. In the birth of short stories Edger Allen Poo played an important role. Short stories may be oral or written. Short stories has always some moral. Short stories are such kinds of stories, which must be readable and completable within thirty minute to one hour. It has its birth before 19th century. Modern Bodo short stories has been first composed by Nilkamal Brahma.

Keywords : Plot, Theme and Technique and Economic Condition.

1.1. Introduction

In general sense, Modernism is considered opposite to post-modernism. It is a unique result of accident and design. "Modernism is completely contradictory to traditional knowledge. It is a new kind of idea having modern characteristics." Modernism leads to social and cultural changes. In other words, it is a product of Globalisation. The concept of Modernism emerged between 19th to 20th century. During that period, most of the people have been influenced by western cultures. For some people, Modernisation means Westernization. Some of the things which are arising as a result of Modernisation are Globalisation, Industrialisation and Social Change.

"One of the main causes of Modernism is mainly as a result of fear of theFirst World War. Modernism mainly rejected the traditional ideas and values." It means replacing the old hand made products and traditional knowledge with machine made products and industries.

The concept of Modernism is reflected in the writings of American poet Ezra Pound. The important works "Make it New" which was published in 1945 has the ideas of modernism reflected in it. It this work, the concept of post-modernism is also reflected. The concept of modernism is also reflected in some short stories like "Odour of Chrysanthenus" by "D.H. Lowrence", "The Gorden Party" by "Katherine Mansifield", "The Mark on the Wall" by "Virgina" and so on.

The concept of Modernism is also reflected in some of the Bodo short stories. To cope up with the Modernisation process, some of the writers has reflected the concept of modernisation in their works. Some of the Bodo short stories in which the concept of Modernism reflected are like "Sirinai Mandar Bibar" and "Gwlwmdwi" by "Nilkamal Brahma".

Other short stories in which the concept of Modernism is reflected are "Kwmshi Durlai" by "Hari Bhushan Brahma" and "Bihamjw Hybrid" by "Nabin Narzari".

The values of Modernism is also reflected in the short story Mwdwi arw Gwlwmdwi, where the writer has used different techniques of Modernism.

Some of the definitions of Modernism given by different scholars are as follows :

According to M.H. Abrams – "The term modernism is widely used to identify new and distinctive features in the subjects from concepts and styles of literature and the arts in the early decade of the present century, but especially after World War I (1914-18). (A Glustory of Literary Terms Book)"

Roger Griffin in his book "The Temporality of the New" has defined Modernism as "Modernism can be defined in a maximalist. Vission as a broad cultural social on political initiative sustained by the ethos."

1.2. Aims and Objective

The main objective of this study is to see the impacts of modernism in Bodo literature like the plot, theme and technique and Economic Condition. We have seen that Modernism has impacted the literature and culture of the Bodos in many different ways. We have seen the impacts of Modernism in different the plot, Theme and technique and economic condition.

1.3. Methodology

In this study, the main methodology used is the analytical method. The Data has been collected from different text books and journals. It is mainly collected from secondary sources.

1.4. Review of Literature

Many literature have been impacted by modernism in the present age. In the same way, we have also seen the impacts of Modernism in different Bodo short stories, poetries and novels.

But unfortunately, the literatures on the impacts of Modernism in Bodo culture and literature is very less. But somehow, the researcher has been able to collect a few of them. Some of them are "Boro Thunlaini Jarimin (History of Bodo Literature)" by Manaranjan Lahary, "Boro Sungdo Soloni Jarimin (History of Bodo Short Stories)" by Rakhao Basumatary, "Nwiji Jouthaini Thunlai Bijirnai" by Dr. Adaram Basumatary, "Society and Culture on Bodo Short Stories" by Dr. Bijit Giri Basumatary, "Sirinai Mandar" by Nilkamal Brahma, "Srimati Durlai" by Haribhushan Brahma, "Boro Sungdo Soloni Bwhwithi Dahar" Edited by Swarna Prabha Chainary, "Solo Bihung"(Part-II) Edited by Boro Thunlai Aphad, "Literary Theory and Criticism" by Patrica Waugh.In these literatures, the impacts of Modernism on different short stories, poetries and novels has been mentioned.

1.5. Statement of the Problem

As a result of Globalisation, we have seen the increasing impact of Modernism in Bodo literature. Today's literature is completely different from traditional literature. Some of the major works where we can find the impacts of modernism in contemporary scenario are:-

"Make it New" by American Poet Ezra Pound, Ulysses by James Joyce, The Wast Land by T.S. Elist, "Odoun of Chrysanthems" by D.H. Lawrence, The Garden Party by Katherine Mansfield, The Mark on the Wall by Virgionia and so on.

Some of the Bodo short stories, where we can find the impacts of Modernism are Sirinai Mandar by Nilkamal Brahma, Mwdwi arw Gwlwmdwi and so on. Apart from that, some of the works where modern techniques have been used are the works of Hari Bhusan Brahma and Nabin Narzary. We can find the different impacts of modernism in these works.

2.1. Plot

In the plot "Sirinai Mandar" by Nilkamal Brahma, it has been stated about the arious problems of the contemporary society like the problems between husband and wife in leading their daily lives as well as financial probem. Apart from that due to the lack of satisfaction of mind, body and spirit, divorce and remarry has become a common issue in contemporary Bodo society now-a-days. Even though traditional Bodo society does not support divorce, but in this age of modernization, it ha become a common phenomenon. But as mentioned in the plot "Sirinai Mandar Bibar" by Nilkamal Brahma, the divorced couple were not getting remarried and had to suffer in grief. In this plot, the impacts of Western culture in Bodo society has also been reflected. Because the things like bodily satisfaction can be found mostly n western cultures.

In another plot "Mwdwi arw Gwlwmdwi" by Nilkamal Brahma, he has mentioned that a cowboy like Gwmbwr, who had to struggle hard for his daily life has turned into a rich industrialist with the help of his wise knowledge. With his strength and vigour, Gwmbwr has turned into a rich industrialist from a cowboy. In this plot, we have seen the impacts of modernization and westernization in Bodo literature, i.e. how a village cowboy like Gwmbwr has turned into a rich city industrialist.

The plot "Bihamjw Hybrid" by Nabin Narzari has also been created mainly by looking at the impacts of modernization and globalisationin Bodo society. In this plot, he has narrated how a modern daughter-in-law like Puspalata has faced problems in adjusting with the traditional Bodo society in her in-law's house. Puspalata is facing problems in traditional food habits, dresses, living style, work and so on. The writer has created many plots based on all these issues.

2.2. Theme and Technique

The short story "Srinai Mandar" by Nilkamal Brahma is written by looking at the ideologies of modernization and westernization and its impacts in Bodo society. It has been written by looking at the characters of up to datequalified girls of modern age like Balengsri. After her marriage, Balengsri cannot satisfy her husband and tried to escape, but has to face with lots of challenges and because of being disliked by everyone has been forced to live in isolation. In this way, we have seen lots of impacts of modernization and westernization in traditional Bodo society, culture and literature. Just like Balengsri, now-a-days, there are many women in Bodo society who has been impacted by western cultures. The main theme of this story is that many up to date qualified girls like Balengsri has been impacted by westernization, who without thinking their future suffered from early marriage followed by divorce and isolation. It is a meesage to the Bodos about the impacts of modernization in traditional Bodo society. The moral of the story is that one has to find out his own way of living.

In the short story "Srimati Durlai" by Haribhushan Brahma, it has been mentioned about the characters of modern Bodo girls. In this story, it has been mentioned about the shameless and courages characters of a girl like Srimati. His ideology and method of writings are remarkeable. Just like Lakshminath Bezbarooah, Haribhushan Brahma is regarded as the Rashraj of Bodo literature. Because he has composed many different types of funny and sweetful short stories.

In the story "Sirinai Mandar" lots of impacts of Modernism has been found. Like it has been highlighted how to cope up with traditional Bodo society and environment.

The short story "Bihamjw Hybrid" by Rabin Narzari has been composed looking at the characters of modern Bodo daughter in laws mainly city dwellers. In this story, the impacts of modernism in traditional Bodo society has been reflected.

In the literature by Nilkamal Brahma, the idea is mainly about the beauties of a girl. In his story, many of the characters of a modern Bodo girl has been reflected. He has sifferent brilliant techniques like dialogue, story-telling and writing. His stories are also having seep philosophies. His writing styles are very remarkeable and attractive. His stories are also very truthful and beautiful. He has created many different short stories just like the transformation of a village life into a city life and so on. He has also created many short stories where the impacts of modernization in Bodo society can be found just like Sirinai Mandar Bibar and Mwdwi arw Gwlwmdwi. His writing techniques are very unique.He has a very unique style of story-telling. He used to tell stories within short time. His writing skills are very brilliant. In the writings of Haribhushan Brahma also, the impacts of Modernism has been reflected.

2.3. Economic Condition

In the short story Mwdwi arw Gwlwmdwi of the book Sirinai Mandar, along with the impacts of modernization, economic development in Bodo society has also been mentioned. In the story, a cowboy called Gwmbwr due to his tireless hard work has developed has become the owner of "Borosa Indi Textile" which characterizes economic development.

Because a cowboy like Gwmbwr Mushahary after being expelled by his village owner Mwnbaru began to search jobs in town. After coming to town, Gwmbwr began working as a woodcutter, thela puller, rickshaw puller, hotel boy and finally after staying in the house of business magent Digambar Basumatary learnt to cultivate Endi with modern technology. After cultivating Endi, he also began selling it and later opened Borosa Endi Textile Farm and also began to expoet it to different places and in that way began earning more and more money. If Gwmbwr continued to live in village, he would have not got that scope. In that way, he has given a meddage to Bodo youths on how to develop one's skill like Gwmbwr.

3.0. Conclusion

From the above discussion, we have learnt about the different impacts of Modernism in Bodo society. From modernism, it has been slowly and gradually upgrading to ultra-modernism. Now a days, we have seen about the different impacts of modernism in Bodo society. Instead of coping up with the traditional Bodo society, people began searching for new ways of life in this age of Globalisation. Modernism is rapidly increasing because of modern technologies. From Modernism, it is developing into modernism and its impacts can be found in Bodo society as well.

The ideology of Modernism began in western literature and slowly and gradually, it began migrating to other literatures including Bodo literature as well. Just like other literatures, the ideology of modernism is transforming to post-modernism in Bodo literature as well. Modernism has brought new techniques to Bodo literature. The Bodo literature has also been frequently impacted by the different waves of modernism.

References

1. Basumatary, Dr. Adaram, Nwiji Jowthaini Thunlai Bijirnai, 2019.
2. Basumatary Dr. Bijitgiri, Society and Culture on Bodo short stories, 2019, August, 1st Edition published by Mrs. Hiramoni Basumatary, Chirang, B.T.A.D. (Assam).
3. Basumatary Rakhao, A history of Bodo short stories, 2013, January, 2nd Edition, words & words, Kokrajhar, Bodoland, India.
4. Brahma, Nilkamal, Sirinai Mandar, 1985 Sijiow Publication Board, Bijni (Assam).
5. Brahma Haribhushan, Srimati Durlai, 2010 August, 2nd Edition, N.L. Publication, Kokrajhar, B.T.C. (Assam)
6. Bodo Thunlai Aphad, Solo Bihung (part II), 2nd Edition 2010, 31 January, Bodo Sahitya Sabha, Kokrajhar.
7. Chainary Swarna Prabha, Boro Sundo Soloni Buhwithi Dahar, 2014 2nd Edition, Sahitya Akademy, Rabindra Bhawan, 35 Firoz

Shah Road, New Delhi 110001.

8. Waugh Patricia, Literary Theory and Criticism, 2006 1st Edition. Oxford University Press. YMCA Library Building, Jaising Road, New Delhi 11001.

CHAPTER TWO

Ideologies Reflected in the Short Story Dumpao's Cake'

Abstract

In the world of Bodo Literature, Sociology has emerged as a new discipline. We have seen that in this age of the 21st century, Globalisation has impacted the Bodo Society in many different ways. In this short story, there is a close relationship between Globalisation and Bodo Society. In the short story "Dumphaoni Pitha" by Janil Kumar Brahma, the nature of contemporary Bodo society like economy, literature and culture has been reflected. In this short story, the different types of mind like positive mind and negative mind has been reflected as well.

Keywords : Future life, Society, Role, Findings.

1.1. Introduction

The book Dumphaoni Pitha by Janil Kumar Brahma is the first short story book in Bodo literature. The book has been published in the year 2005. In this book, some of the recurring incidents in Contemporary Bodo Society has been mentioned. The story is based on an incident which had taken place at Samthaibari village market. Later, the incident has taken its form of a modern Bodo short story. In this story, a Bodo women named Dumphao had to sell pitha (traditional Bodo rice cake) at Samtaibari market to lead her family. After that, the women had also purchased sweeing machine to stitch clothes in the market. Apart from that, Dumphao had also helped her husband named Somen, who is a teacher by profession, in his social works. The social work includes the roles like protection, promotion and preservation of cultures, customs, traditions and so on. Apart from that, it also includes construction of martyr's tomb of those people, who sacrificed their lives in the movement for promotion, protection and preservation of their cultures, customs, traditions, languages, literatures and so on. It also includes the role played by Dhumphao for empowering women in Bodo society.

1.2. Aim and Objectives

In this discussion, we are going to discuss the future of Bodo society as well as its recurring events in the society and how its going to impact the society. It also includes what type of role an women has to play for the empowerment of women in Bodo society.

1.3. Methods

In this discussion, analytical methods have been used. In the collection of data both primary and secondary sources are used. The main books (Text book) have been used as primary sources and the criticism books have been used as the secondary source of data.

1.4. Review of Literature

In the field of this type of criticism we do not able to find much literary criticism. In their books some author's criticized about this subject but these are not enough. But they donot able to give complete description. The Ideologies reflect of this type of criticism can be find in "Boro Sungdo Soloni Jarimin" of Rakhao Basumatary, "Literary Theory and Criticism" of Waugh Patricia. But with this books the criticism do not fulfill. Therefore to know a literature widely or completely the criticism of literature is essential. This literary criticism will help to know the literature widely.

2.1. Future Life

Each and every human beings have an aim or dream of building their future life. Some dreams are successful, while others are unsuccessful. It depends upon his work. In the same way, in the story Dumpaoni Pitha by Janil Kumar Brahma, the aim of an woman named Dumpao has been reflected. In this story, "Dumpao thought that if women from other communities can open and run tea stalls, then why not Bodo women as they are also human beings ?."[1] Based on the ideology of Dumpao, the concept of women empowerment in Bodo society has been narrated in this short story and its one of the means to encourage Bodo women. As in this story, the success as well as fruits of Dumpao's labour has been mentioned. In this story, it has also been mentioned that Dumpao's thought has succeded into reality. In this story, a women named Dumpao had first of all opened a tea stall at Samtaibari market and later opened a tailoring shop. In her tailoring shop, Dumpao had brought many Bodo young men and women into her shop to make them learn tailoring. Apart from that with her profit, later she also donated money for the construction of martyr's tomb, who sacrificed their valuable lives for the protection, promotion and preservation of their cultures. It is one of the steps adopted by Dumpao to encourage the future generation. In that way, the idea of dream and success has been mentioned in this short story. But other girls in the short story called Gaodang and Sarala is not seen thinking about her future. Dumpao's husband Somen, who is a teacher by profession is also seen thinking about the future generation in this short story. In this story, it has been mentioned about the role played by him in the protection, promotion and preservation of their language.

2.2. Types of Mind

According to sociologist and psychologist, two types of mind can be found, which has been reflected in this short story. They are positive mind and negative mind. It has been discussed below.

Positive Mind : In this story, the positive mind of a Bodo women like Dumphao has been reflected. In this story, a Bodo women named Dumpao had to sell pitha (traditional Bodo rice cake) at Samtaibari market to lead her family. After that, the women had also purchased sweeing machine to stitch clothes in the market. Apart from that, Dumpao had also helped her husband named Somen, who is a teacher by profession, in his social works. The social work includes the roles like protection, promotion and preservation of cultures, customs, traditions

and so on. Apart from that, it also includes construction of martyr's tomb of those people, who sacrificed their lives in the movement for promotion, protection and preservation of their cultures, customs, traditions, languages, literatures and so on. It also includes the role played by Dumpao for empowering women in Bodo society.

In this story, "Dumphao thought that if women from other communities can open and run tea stalls, then why not Bodo women as they are also human beings ?"[2] Based on the ideology of Dumphao, the concept of women empowerment in Bodo society has been narrated in this short story and its one of the means to encourage Bodo women. As in this story, the success as well as fruits of Dumphao's labour has been mentioned. In this story, it has also been mentioned that Dumphao's thought has succeded into reality. In this story, a women named Dumphao had first of all opened a tea stall at Samtaibari market and later opened a tailoring shop. In her tailoring shop, Dumphao had brought many Bodo young men and women into her shop to make them learn tailoring. Apart from that with her profit, later she also donated money for the construction of martyr's tomb, who sacrificed their valuable lives for the protection, promotion and preservation of their cultures. It is one of the steps adopted by Dumphao to encourage the future generation. In that way, the idea of dream and success has been mentioned in this short story. But another girl in the short story called Sarala is not seen thinking about her future. Dumphao's husband Somen, who is a teacher by profession is also seen thinking about the future generation in this short story. In this story, it has been mentioned about the role played by him in the protection, promotion and preservation of their language.

Negative Mind : In this short story, the negative mind of Bodo girls like Gaodang and Sarala has also been reflected. The phrases like married with which boy, what type of luck, asking to seek jobs in town, better to die has been reflected in the characters of Bodo girls like Gaodang and Sarala.

2.3. Society

This short story is mainly based on the recurring events in contemporary Bodo society. In this short story, the things of contemporary Bodo society like village, culture, town, culture and economy has been reflected. The recurring domestic problems in contemporary Bodo society has been reflected in this short story. "The phrases like where is the bread earned by you, no job, no service and so on reflects the recurring events in contemporary Bodo society. In this story, we can find different things like social work; promotion, protection and preservation of Bodo culture; empowerment of Bodo women and so on."[3]

One has to do different works to lead his or her lives in contemporary society. It has been reflected in this story. In this story, a Bodo women named Dumphao had to sell pitha (traditional Bodo rice cake) at Samtaibari market to lead her family. After that, the women had also purchased sweeing machine to stitch clothes in the market. Apart from that, Dumphao had also helped her husband named Somen, who is a teacher by profession, in his social works. The social work includes the roles like protection, promotion and preservation of cultures, customs, traditions and so on. Apart from that, it also includes construction of martyr's tomb of those people, who sacrificed their lives in the movement for promotion, protection and preservation of their cultures, customs, traditions, languages, literatures and so on. It also includes the role played by Dumphao for empowering women in Bodo society.

2.4. Roles

Apart from her role, in this story it is also seen that Dumphao has been helping her husband Somen, who is a teacher by profession in his social works. Apart from leading her family, Dumphao was also opening and running a tea stall to earn their daily bread as reflected in this short story. Since her husband's job is not regularized, Dumphao was compelled to do these jobs. Somen is also a social worker apart from his profession. But Gaodang and Sarala were not seen doing such kind of works.

2.5. Findings

From the above discussion, we can find that a women like Dumphao had been successfully transforming her dream into reality. She has been playing a leading role in serving her family as well as society. She is also seen helping her husband in his social works like promotion, protection and preservation of one's culture, customs, languages, traditions and so on.

4.0. Conclusion

In this short story, the different things in contemporary Bodo society like environment, economy, society, protection of culture, language and literature has been reflected. Apart from that, the role played by Dumphao in empowering women in Bodo society has also been mentioned.

References :

1. Brahma, Janil Kumar; Dumphaoni Pitha (2005); Onsumwi Library, RNB Road, Kokrajhar, BTR Assam.
2. Basumatary, Rakhao; Boro Sungdo Soloni Jarimin (5 February 2013); Words and Words, Kokrajhar, Bodoland, India.
3. Waugh, Patricia, Literary Theory and Criticism Oxford University Press, YMCA Library Building. Jai Singh Road, New Delhi 110001. First Indian Edition 2006.

CHAPTER THREE

Traditional Bodo Culture and Society as Reflected in the Short Story 'Hangma Hangsani Agor Phali'

Abstract

In this work, the different traditional items of Bodo Society has been mentioned. Just like traditional folk song, dresses, social philosophy, and culture. Without the help of social philosophy, the researcher is trying to protect, promote and preserve all these traditions. The short story Hangma Hangsani Agor Fali is based on the traditional cultures of the Bodos like dresses, attires and so on. In this short story, major reflections on Bodo culture has been made as well as how these cultures are going to loode in this age of modernization. Each and every material as well as non-material culture has been reflected in this short story like musical instruments, dresses and so on. Apart from that, the traditional rural life in Bodo society has also been reflected. The different musical instruments like jews harp, flute, as well as traditional dresses, music, songs, cultures, customs and traditions of the Bodo society has been reflected. Different traditional norms of the Bodo society like seeking a daughter in law, seeking a bride, cow boy, maid servant and so on has been reflected.

Kywords : Folk Song, Traditional attires, Society and Culture.

1.1. Introduction

In this discussion, the works of Jwishri Boro has been reviewed. The book won the Sahitya Akademi Award in the year 2011. In this short story, the different cultural traditions as well as the traditional folk songs of Bodo society has been reflected. The main discussion in this short story is about the happiness and sadness in romance. This short story is mainly based on the love between Nawati and Sonaram. The traditional Bodo practices like a girl used to present traditional attires to their love ones during Bwisagu festival has been reflected in this short story. But the romance success in someone's case while it fails in other's case. In this short story, the failure of the romance between Nawati and Sonaram has been reflected and Nawati was compelled to present her traditional attire to a boy named Rindao, who has just passed his PU exam and Rindao hugged her in love.

1.2. Aim and Objectives

The main discussion in this short story is about the traditional folk songs, attires, society and culture.

1.3. Method

In this study, both analytical as well as traditional methods have been used. The data is based on primary as well as secondary sources like books, personal interviews and so on.

1.4. Literary Criticism

In this discussion, the traditional folk songs, attires and cultures of the Bodos have been elaborated.

1.5. Importance

There is a lot of importance in this discussion about Bodo traditions and cultures.

2.1. Folk Song

Folk Song in traditional Bodo society is a kind of song which we have inherited it from our forefathers. It is a song which is sung with the help of traditional musical instruments or sometimes even without music. Folk song has some unique characters like it has no writers or composers. It is a traditional knowledge of the Bodos. In the story by Jwishri Boro, the traditional attires as well as folk songs has been reflected.

The folk song reflected in this short story is

Bari Khonani Ouwa Bijouyao Bananwi
Kouyou Kouyou Dao Kouyou Gabdwng
Ouwa Bilaiya Sifung Sudwng
Batha Bibungya Jotha Damdwng
Barlangfa Kham Damdwng
Bardwi Sikwla Mwsadwng
Nwngkou Gwsw Khangnanwi Angbwsw Bwdwr Jadwng
Ada Sonaram Gajwla Angni Ernai Agorao Khana Nangdwn
(By Staying in the bamboo tree to the corner near my home
Crying khoukhou khoukhou khoukhou.
The bamboo leaves are playing flute
The batha is playing jotha.
Barlangfa is playing the Khaam
Bardwi chikha is dancing
I have gone wild thinking you
Brother Sonaram while making attire gets mistake thinking you.
)

The crying of a cuckoo bird in the environment marks the natural beginning of a new year (Bwisagu) in Bodo society. Bwisagu is a traditional spring time festival of the Bodos which is often considered to be traditional new year in Bodo society. During that time a type of strong winds known as Bardwi Sikwla (also called Bordoichila) used to blow.

All these signs of nature marks the beginning of a Bwisagu. The Bodo young man and women use to sing and dance during the Bwisagu festival by singing folk songs and using traditional musical instruments like kham, sifhung, sherja and jotha as well as by wearing traditional attires. The Bodo young women also used to present traditional attires to their loved ones (especially Bodo young men) on the Bwisagu festival.

In this short story, the romance of Nabati and Sonaram has been reflected. While weaving, Nabati has been always thinking of Sonaram. Nabati has been thinking of presenting the traditional attire to Sonaram during Bwisagu festival. She has also been requesting him to visit her during Bwisagu festival. In this short story, in this way, the story of a romance and traditional norms has been reflected. In the Bwisagu festival, the Bodo youths use to express their feelings among each other. They used to share and express their feelings and thoughts to their loved ones.

It has been through Sonaram's words in the story.

"Deglai Jala Agwi Deglai Jala
Deglai Haslabkala
Pwigou Bwisagyao Nwngkou Ang Langfwitargwn
Nwnglo Tiyari Takha."

(In this year its too late
I will be surely coming to
Take you in the year
You just get ready)

In this short story, through this folk song, the idea of love and marriage in Bodo society has been reflected. In this short story, Sonaram has promised to marry Nabati in the next Bwisagu as it has became too late in this Bwisagu.

In this way, there are many other folk songs in Bodo society, which we have inherited from our forefathers.

2.2. Traditional Attires

In this short story, Nabati had tried to present traditional attire to Sonaram during the Bwisagu festival. As mentioned in this short story, the Bodo young women used to present traditional attire to their loved ones (specially Bodo young man) during the Bwisagu festival. Just like Nabati, it was the tradition of the Bodo women to weave traditional attires. It was mandatory to have traditional knowledge of weaving for the Bodo girls specially during those days. Some of the traditional attires of the Bodos include Dokhona, Aronai, Fasra, Gamosha, Jwmgra and so on. It was a traditional knowledge as well as habit of Bodo women and the Bodo women always use to prepare and keep it ready before the Bwisagu festival to send it to their loved ones during the Bwisagu.

2.3. Society

In this short story, the village lives of traditional Bodo society has been reflected. Some of them are just like village life, love between cowboy and maid servant, seeking bride or daughter in law and so on. Just like Nabati's father had seek a son-in-law who is having a job, but since he came to know that he is under matric, so he left. These are some of the recurring events in contemporary Bodo society.

Apart from that, the traditional cultures, festivals, attires and musical instruments in Bodo society has also been highlighted. Some of the practices like presenting traditional attires to their loved ones during Bwisagu has also been reflected.

2.4. Material Culture

In this short story, the material culture like traditional attires, musical instruments like Kham, Sifung, Sherja and Jotha has been highlighted.

2.5. Social Culture

In this short story, some of the traditional practices of the Bodo society has been highlighted like presenting traditional attires to their loved ones during Bwisagu, singing folk songs by using traditional musical instruments and so on.

3.0. Conclusion

In this short story, the traditional Bodo society and cultures has been reflected. Just like presenting traditional attires to loved ones during Bwisagu, singing folk songs and so on. In this short story, many traditional beliefs and practices have also been highlighted. In this short story, the material culture like traditional attires, musical instruments like Kham, Sifung, Sherja and Jotha has been highlighted. In this short story, some of the traditional practices of the Bodo society has been highlighted like presenting traditional attires to their loved ones during Bwisagu, singing folk songs by using traditional musical instruments and so on. Apart from that, the traditional cultures, festivals, attires and musical instruments in Bodo society has also been highlighted. Some of the practices like presenting traditional attires to their loved ones during Bwisagu has also been reflected.

References

1. Basumatary, Rakhao, Boro Sungdo Soloni Jarimin, words & words, Kokrajhar, Bodoland, India, 2nd Edition (2013)
2. Boro Joyshri, Jiu Saharani Beduin, Words and Words, R.N.B. Road, Kokrajhar, Bodoland, 2nd Edition, November (2015)
3. Waugh, Patricia, Literary Theory and Criticism, Published by Oxford University Press, YMCA Library Building, Jai Singh Road, New Delhi, India, 110001. Fins 1st Edition 2006.

CHAPTER FOUR

A Study on the History of the Bodo Short Story (Since-2000-2010)

Abstract

In the context of Bodo literature, the number of Bodo short stories has been increasing at contemporary times. The number of short stories kept on increasing at present. Before discussion in this paper, age of literary period has been considered to study the development of short stories in Bodo literature. It has discussed the trend, tendencies, theme and society of the Bodo short stories. In this paper, it has discussed the development of short stories in Bodo literature from 2000 to 2010. Prior to that, it is also to discuss the origin of short stories in Bodo literature. In the main of discussion, it has discussed about the development of short stories in Bodo literature from 2000 to 2010. It will now discuss about the short stories in Bodo literature published between 2000 to 2010.

Keywords : Trends, Writers, Books

1.1 : Introduction

Before 19th century a prominent Porasi writer Mopasa has penned down the initial short story. In collaboration with Mopasa, Plastor has taught how to perceive new life through short story.Following them, short story of some writers began to appear in literature of different languages of the world. Russia's Maxim

Gorky, Sekob, Gogol Liu, Tolstoy, Ivan, Turgenev, England's Robertluie, Stevenson, Ponred, Kipoli, America's Erton, Edgar Alanpo, Henry, William Soseton and India's Premchandra, Rabindra Nath Tagore and writers of small literatures of different places have founded the story literature. In Assamese literature, Laksminath Bezbaruahas found a short story by welcoming western literature. Thus, in Bodo literature as well, Ishan Mushahary has founded a short story by writing 'Abari'. Prior to that, with the help of Mopasa, Promod Chandra Brahma has composed a short story of 'Rondasa Pagli'. However, this story did not clearly appear. Therefore, though it was first in composition but 'Abari' was literally accepted as short story. Abari story was appeared in 'Alongbar' magazine composed by Promod Chandra Brahma in 1938. Thereafter, some writers began to write a story. Followed by, 'Bobi' a story of Prasanjit Brahma has appeared in 'Fungkha' magazine.

The short story was composed Gohen Basumary's Un Daha in Monorojon Lahary's edition souvenir Okapwr after the formation of Bodo literary society in 1952. After that the introduction of short story is increasing gradually in the Bodo literature. Their stories are Barhungkani Unao written by Monoronjon Lahary, Fwimal Mijing by Chittaranjan Mushahary, Hagra Guduni Mwi by Nilkamal Brahma, Srimati Durlai by Haribasan Brahma, Hongla Pandit of Katindra Swrgoyary, Dumpaoni Pitha by Janil Kumar Brahma, Mister Hybridni Gwlwmdwi Arw Mwdwi of J.D. Basumatary, Sonani Dera of Leben Lal Mwshahary, Jiu Saharani Bedwin of Jwisri Boro etc.

Now a days, in the Bodo literature the short story of Bodos are rapidly increasing.Because within short period the writers and readers are mostly capturing the creativity idea of the Bodo short stories. As a result the number of short story is increasing. Mentioning of short story is not possible. Therefore, here decided to discuss the short stories which have written during the period from 2000 to 2020.

1. 2. Aim and Objectives

The main aim and objective is to study the new perspective of the Bodo short story and its related trend and tendencies. These leave vast scope of study for one to undertake research work and help to preserve the traditional culture of great Bodo Society.

From the above discussion the following are the sorted list of aims and objectives of the proposed research:

- To discussed regarding the trends of the Bodo short stories
- To mention the writers.
- To highlight the books of the short story.

1.3. Methodology

This criticism has been done through analytical method. In the collection of data both primary and secondary sources are used. The main books (Text book) have been used as primary sources and the criticism books, magazine, Journal and thesis have been used as the secondary source of data.

1.4. Study of the Area

The areas of the study of the research will be a study of the Bodo Short Stories Since 2000 to 2010. The Bodo constitute a very important section of different group and races with their distinct culture and linguistics traits. Therefore, the study is taken to study the short stories written during the period of 2000 to 2010.

1.5. Review of Literature

In the field of this type of criticism we do not able to find much literary criticism. In their books some author's criticized about this subject but these are not enough. But they don't able to give complete description. The modern reflection of this type of criticism can be find in "History of Boro Literature" of critic Monoranjan Lahary. "A History of Boro Literature" of Madhuram Boro. "A History of Bodo short stories" of Rakao Basumatary, "Nwjwr and Shanshri" of Bijitgiri Basumatary, "A history & a criticism of Bodo Literature" of Raju Kr. Brahma, "Society and culture on Bodo short stories of Dr. Bijitgiri Basumatary, "Boro Sungdo Soloni Bwhwithi Dahar" of Sarna Prabha Chainary (Edited), " Nwiji Jouthaini Thunlai Bijirnai" of Dr. Adaram Basumatary, "Impact of Modernity on Bodo culture as reflected in Boro short stories" of Dr. Rupnath Owary, "Modern Criticism and Theory" of Lodge David & Wood Nigel (Edited, "Literary Theory and criticism" of Patrica Waugh and others book. But with these books the criticism do not fulfill.Therefore to know a literature widely or completely the criticism of literature is essential. This literary criticism will help to know the literature widely.

2.0. Trends, Writers, Books

2.1. From 2000 to 2002

Arabinda Uzir has edited a book called "Athumse Sungdo Solo" in 2000. He has edited this book by collecting a total of 20 old and new Bodo short stories.

In the book "Jaorikhangnai Sungdo Solo" by Khatindra Swargiary, there are a collection of nine Bodo short stories. This book has been published in the year 2000. The short stories are as follows: 1. Sanjoufu ni Radab. 2. Gorse Goli. 3. Jahab Bondho. 4. Jaorikhangnai Gibi Aida. 5. Silingkhar. 6. Garbwnai Bwtwrni Mwnse Sketch. 7. Anan Gosaini Noao. 8. Kargil Daoha and 9. Sangrema.

Rupendra Lahary's bok "Binanao Gwdwi" has been published in the year 2000. In this book, there are a collection of 5 Bodo short stories. They are as follows: 1. Lorhainai Loveni Rega. 2.

They are as follows: 1. Lorhainai Loveni Rega. 2. Jiuni Laithun 3. Fagunni Jaoliya Barjwng. 4. Binanao Gwdwi and 5. Gwdan Mijing.

The book "No One Thirteen File" by Dharpajit Basumatary has been published in 2000. The book has been published by Sijou Publication. There are eight (8) no. of short stories in this book. They are as follows: 1. Gongse Laijam. 2.Mwdwmnai sandni Mwnamnai. 3. Mwnse Diary. 4. Presentation. 5. Thakwmanai Isara. 6. No one Thirteen file. 7. Baiglinai Gwswni Baiflenai Mijing and 8. Dorsi Hor.

The book "Suami Angni" by Nani Gopal Brahma is a famous short story book published in 2000. In this book, there are only three (3) short stories. They are as follows: 1. Jwngklini Jwngklwb Jiu. 2. Kokrajharni Kochin Sim and 3. Suami Angni.

The book "Miss Jarou" by Rohin Rindao Borosa was published in 2000. The short story "Benw Sinaiti" is the first work by Diganta

Lahary. Diganta Lahary is one of the best fictional writer.The work by Diganta Lahary was published in the year 2000.

Some of the Bodo short stories published in the year 2001 are discussed below:

The short story book "Ombashi Fung" by Urkhao Gwra Brahma is a very famous short story book.The book "Jwngni Solo" is a short story book edited by Mogesh Narzary. The book consists of twelve (12) Bodo short stories which are: 1. Modod by Dalsing Basumatary. 2. Rwjabwi Mung Jouthaini Soloao Suku Thangki by Khatindra Swargiary. 3. Gamwnni Thakwi by Rituraj Basumatary. 4. Embu Sitroni Udangshri by Biseswar Basumatary. 5. Bima by Gwjwn Khungur. 6. Jaikhlongni Songshar by Toreswar Basumatary. 7. Rugung Mwnwi Dinga by Nipen Chandra Baglary. 8. Obotira Jiu by Diyan Chandra Basumatary. 9. Sansrini Lwitwyao by Bhupen Chandra Narzary. 10. Mwnabilini Dengkhw by Uttam Chandra Brahma. 11. Simangyao Bidi Jagwn by Arabinda Uzir and 12. Daosri Athing by Mogesh Narza Boro.

The short story "Madori" written by Girish Kachari was published in 2001.

The three short story books by Binanda Swargiary are as follows: 1. Kouseni Dengkhw Hor Gejerni Phone Jinjiri. In this book, there are a total of 18 short stories. It has been published by Onsumwi Library.

In the book "Jokaitham Dwngse" by Bijay Baglary, there are a total of thirteen short stories. It has been published by Sonitpur District Boro Thunlai Afad.

The book "Gwdan Jarimin" created by Debendra Boro has been published in 2001.

The book "Rwmwnai Barse Bibar" by Sailen Basumatary has been published in 2001. There are a total of ten (10) short stories in this book. They are as follows: 1. Rwmwnai Barse Bibar. 2. Sombarini Daha. 3. Unni Jwnwmao. 4. Dwbwilangnai San. 5. Bihamjw Gaojru. 6. Certificate. 7. Faguni. 8. Mijingni Habila. 9. Haranggani Adra and 10. Dwisari.

The short story book "Mainao" by Ronira Sangra Ramchiary has been published in 2001. The book has been published by Kishori Ramchiary. There are a total of six (6) short stories in this book. They are: 1. Rickshawala. 2. Boro Hinjao. 3. Khwmsini Saogari. 4. Mainao. 5. Address and 6. Bishni Twrsi.

The Book Bwhwiti Dahar Published in 2002:

The book "Obe Nenai Dalanga Baigrebnaisw" by Bodo funny short story writer Nandeswar Daimary consists of thirteen (13) short stories. They are as follows: 1. AIDS. 2. Laitikh. 3. Obe Nenai Dalanga Baigrebnai. 4. Mandar Bibarni Daha. 5. Hawkerni Kerosine. 6. Ojod. 7. Pwisali. 8. Ramwndaya Bwrwiba Mwnbaodwng. 9. Aluri. 10. Projectni Gubun Mwnse Mung. 11. Kamani. 12. Tangnaini Daoha. 13. Tution Master.

Monsoon Lahary commented about these short stories: All these stories are good to read and listen. These short stories has been divided into three parts: these are Plot, character and presentation.

The short story book "Geremsha" by Dalsing Basumatary has been published in 2002. There are a total of twelve short stories in this book.

In the book "Bwdwr Baoli Gwsw" by Mukut Prasad Boro, there are a collection of fourteen (14) short stories. They are as follows: 1. Mwnse Suicide Note. 2. Hot list. 3. Diskar. 4. Dukuni Songsar. 5. Sukuni Mijing. 6. Pinnai Gwywi Swngthi. 7. Garbwnai Sanfwrkou Naigirnanwi. 8. Bwdwr Baoli Gwsw. 9. Somaikira. 10. Daha Hangma. 11. Swdwmshri. 12. Felengni Daha. 13. Felengni Daha. 14. Onlainaini Jiu.

In the book "Fagunni Sansekali" by Dhanendra Boro, there are a total of ten (10) short stories. They are as follows: 1. Daohayao Datangswi. 2. Gwrwntiya Swrni. 3. Ako-Fako. 4. Rwnti Lama. 5. Fagunni Sansekali. 6. Customer. 7. Felengni Bandi. 8. Falanggiri. 9. Gas Gwswdwlwng. And 10. Daobaiyari Daobainai Som.

The book "Udang Bwtwrni Daokouyou" by Sanilal Basumatary has been published in the year 2000. There are a total of nine (9) short stories in this book. They are as follows: 1. Udang Bwtwrni Daokouyou. 2. Bajwi Jenggaoni Apsos. 3. Canvass. 4. Voluntiary

Retirement: Megon Mwdwi. 5. Break Dance. 6. Fithai. 7. Model Schoolni Buhut. 8. Satbangsha and 9. Dwlw.

The book "Katase Solo" has been written by Arabinda Uzir.

The short story book "Hor Gejerni Phone" by Binanda Swargiary is a remarkeable one.There are a total of elephant (11) short stories in this book. They are as follows: 1. Hor Gejerni Phone. 2. Falangi Pressure. 3. Bedlao. 4. Fao Fandaisula. 5. Nijari. 6. Bwisaguni Mijing. 7. Lijsuli Rangkini. 8. Daina and 9. Lorhainai Bibarni Mase Sikiri.

The edited book by Bodo Publication Board is a famous collection of short stories. It has been edited in two volumes. In the first book, there is elephant (11) story from Bengali language, one (1) story from Assamese language, four (4) story from Urdu language, two (2) story from Sindhi language, two (2) story from Punjabi language, one (1) story from Dogri language and three (3) story from Hindi language. There are a total of about twenty four (24) short stories.

There are a total of nineteen (19) short stories in the second volume. In this volume, the short stories have been collected and translated from different literatures like Western, South-East Asia, Europe, America and Latin America. It is one of the most remarkable book in Bodo literature. The short stories has been translated from different languages.

The book "Mayani Songsar" by Hareswar Basumatary has been published in 2002.

The book "Somaikira" by Rupendra Lahary and "Kwirwm Dwirwm" by Arun Khungur Borgoyary has been published by Onsumwi Library.

The two short story books created by Dhireswar Boro are "Mandar Bibar (2002)" and "Si Nagirlu Si (2002)". In the book "Mandar Bibar", there are ten (10) short stories. They are as follows:- 1. Mandar Bibar. 2. Sikhla Randi. 3. Bhasis. 4. Simang. 5. Nerswn. 6. Krishnasura Jebwla Siriyw. 7. Mogase. 8. Jwmwi. 9. Ukundwi and 10. Pap arw Udrainai.

In the book "Si Nagirlu Si", there are a collection of ten (10) short stories. They are as follows:- 1. Si Nagirlu Si. 2. Lama Swngthi.

3. Jw Bika Adra Janai Jiu Solo. 4. Barse Golap Barnaimwn. 5. Gubun Mung Thwinai. 6. Oulinai Borofya Simang Nuyw Hajwni Bisombi. 7. Dandiseni Sanmwndangthi and 8. Asinni Gwhwm. Another book by Dhireswar Boro is "Rongni Ri". In this book, there are 11 short stories.

Some other short story books are "Tebgang Oja" by Dhananjoy Basumatary, "Onjalini Laijam" by Binanda Swargiary, "Phutlani Solo" by Anil Kumar Brahma, "Mwjang Hinjao Nagernanwi" by Hejen Ramchiary, "Bala Hamani Bikayao Dokorse Bibarbari" by Debendra Boro, "Dyansorai" by Polai Basumatary.

The short story book "Tinanwi Dwnnai Dobani Goi" by Rokendra Basumatary has been published in 2002.

2.2 : From 2003 to 2005

Some of the books published in the year 2003 are mentioned below:-

The short story book "Post Modernni Plot Sungdannanwi" by Sunil Pukhan Basumatary is a post modern Bodo short story book. The book "Boro Thunlaini Jarimin (History of Bodo literature)' has been created by Manoranjan Lahary.

The short story book "Gaodang" by Indramalati Narzary is a self published book. This book consists of twelve (12) short stories.

The short story book "Hadan" by Nabin Mollo Boro has been published in 2003. It has been published by N.L. Publication. There are) twelve 12) short stories in this book.

The short story book "Mwnda" by Rajen Basumatary has been published in the year 2003. It consists of eight (8) short stories. The stories are as follows: 1. Hongla Masterni Bohari. 2. Doctorate Gaide Brahma. 3. Sukurbar Hataini Daola Berha. 4. Somaini Jwr. 5. Asokanda. 6. Hawasini Bar. and 7. Flop Wickiniser Priced.

The short story "Guma Gwthao" is the first book by Subodh Goyari. It has been published by Onsumwi Library.

The book "Modern Bodo Short Story" which has been edited by Joy Khanta Sarma consists of elephant (11) short stories. It has been published by Sahitya Akademi.

The short story book “Garbwnai Sanfwrkou Nagirnanwi” by Mukut Prasad Boro is the second book by him. It consists of elephant (11) short stories.

The short story book “Solo Bibar” by Bijay Baglary been published in the year 2003. It consists of thirteen (13) short stories. It has been published by Sonitpur District Bodo Literary Society.

The book “Somaj Sibiyari” by Khuntlai Khungur Boro has been published by N.L. Publication. Other short story book published in the year 2003 are “Mwdwini Besena Boha” by Sohaisuli Brahma, “Bilai Rwdwmfinnai Dalai” by Dhwpmani Boro, “Angni Soloao Monalisa” by Hargovind Gayary, “Hangmani Dera” by Rupali Swargiary, “Maisarini Mwdwi” by Hirendra Kumar Narzary, “Abari” by Dwipen Mwchahary, “Swrjilangnai Bibar” by Digol Lahary.

The book “Bajwi Srimati” by Sunil Pukhan Basumatary has been published in the year 2000. It has been printed at Bodosa Press, Kokrajhar.

The short story “Baikwnda Sata arw Laothi Gojo” by Suniti Narzary has been published in the form of a book. It has been published by Haina Publication Guwahati – 36. There are nine (9) stories in this book.

The short story book “Siklani Kelengkari” by Roshen Mwchahary and Dwimasa Brahma has been published by J.N. Publication. It has been published in the year 2003.

Some of the Bodo short story books which has been published in the year 2004 are mentioned below:

The book “Neosijanai Bwrli” by Aron Raja is a remarkeable Bodo short story book. It consists of eight (8) short stories. The short stories are: 1. Jilit. 2. Hor Gejerni Traged. 3. Jinir. 4. Gwrbwni Hojikrounai. 5. Silingkar Sainasali. 6. Sabukh. 7. Neosijanai Bwrli and 8. Latikho. It has been published by Bithorai Library.

In the book “Udang Bwtwrni Jaoliya Bar” by Promortosh Basumatary, there are a total of elephant (11) short stories. They are as follows: 1. Dagi. 2. Batra. 3. Udang Bwtwrni Jaoliya Bar. 4. Jahorlong. 5. Gwrbwni Radai. 6. Bihari Som. 7. Khwmsi Horni Okwafwr Sinaithi. 8. Mijing arw Dwngse Lama. It has been published by Sijou Publication.

The book "Jothai Bidang eba Jothai Solo" has been edited by Gwgwm Brahma Kochary in the year 2004. There are sixteen (16) stories in this book. They are as follows: 1. Fangnwi Narengkol Biphang. 2. Gwdan Slogan. 3. Jamni Bilai. 4. Bangra. 5. Narkhw and some others.

In the book "Alasi" by Gopinath Borgoyary, there are thirteen (13) short stories.

The book "Haina Muli" has been written by Rupendra Lahary.

The book "Badua" written by Upen Chandra Owary has been published by Anu Owary. It consists of fifteen (15) short stories.

The bbook "Sikri Fagla" by Rwmba Owary is a good short story book. It has been published by Biju Prasad Mwchahary.

The book "Mwiratikhi" has been edited by Bijay Baglary. It consists of thirteen (13) short stories. It has been published by Sonitpur District Bodo Literary Society. Other Bodo short stories published in the year 2004 are "Jambi Sikla" by Panidhar Basumatary and "Bajwini Mosla" by Sansuma Khungur Boro.

Some of the Bodo short story books published in the year 2005 are mentioned below:

The book "Iyunni Solo" by Bhupendra Narayan Basumatary has a self-published book. The book "Gwswm Fwisali" by Oron Raja is also an important short story book. This book has been published by Pohimnw Basumatary.

The book "Bwisagini Agor" is written by Indramala Narzary.

The book "Jinjir" has been written by Purnima Swargiary in 2005. It has been published by Bijni College Students Union.

Bidya Sagar Narzary is an important icon in Bodo literature. In his high school days itself, he has written a prose called "Ang Baonw Haya". His short story book is "Urang Farang". There are ten (10) short stories in this book.

The book "Gwdan Mijing" by Mongkorlal Boro is a very important book. It has been published in the year 2005.

The book "Sonani Dera" by Lebenlal Mwchahary has been published in the year 2005. It has been printed and published by

Gwthumni Bod Stall. It consists of twelve (12) stories.

The book "Laodum Sonsrani Jolonga" written by Badal Basumatary is an important book. It has been published by Swargeswari Basumatary.

The book "Dwimu Master" by Lohit Chandra Boro has been published in the year 2005.

The book "Sikri Sikla" by Subodh Gayary has been published in the year 2005. It has been published by Onsumwi Library.

The book "Songbidhan" by Panidhar Choudhury has been published in the year 2005. Another book "Jiflenai Jiuni Saogir" Sabiram Boro has also been published in the year 2005. It has been published by Jaoliya Moholiya.

The book "Dumpaoni Pitha" by Janil Kumar Brahma is a well-known book. It has been published by Sijou Publication. There are fifteen (15) short stories in this book. They are: 1. Dumpaoni Pitha. 2. Alasi. 3. Or. 4. Laishrwnni Bwswr. 5. Rego Dahwna. 6. Dodere Rumbangni Jiu Dahar. 7. 16 Novemberni Aronai. 8. Mansi Gidir: Sonaramni Jiu Lama. 9. Bangkoni Gan Talim: Anwi Sonaisini Usunda. 10. Uwal. 11. Tikiramni Fwimal Mijing: Hwnnanwi Bungnaiywi Ang. 12. Pobesrani Bihamjw.

The book "Se minuteni Local Solo" by Lakshminath Brahma is an important Bodo short story book.

The book "Mister Hybridni Gwlwmdwi arw Mwdwi" by J.D. Basumatary has been published in the year 2005. It comprises of 32 short stories.

The book "Gorse Fwisa" by Madhuram Boro is a collection of short stories.

Some other short story books published in the year 2005 are as follows: "Dustbinni Bibar" by Dhirju Jyoti Basumatary, "Dokona Gangse Baidwngmwn" by Sagram Choudhury, "Bwigri Su" by Hatorkhi Fagla.

Dakhwn. 12. Thwi. 13. Good Morning. 14. Fifit Fifit. 15. Santhi. 16. Deolao. 17. Jati. 18. Pura Terojon. 19. Koro Matha and 20. Certificate.

The book "Malo Driver" by Taren Boro is a composed book. It consists of twentyone (21) short stories. They are as follows: 1. Dhubri Passenger. 2. Hor Gejerni Hatorkhi. 3. Jwlwini Hangar. 4. Shillong product. 5. Dadagiri. 6. Human Rights. 7. Transfer. 8. Master Race. 9. Bima Bhatul. 10. Surrender. 11. Air Hostess. 12. Mykeleak Rwisumwi. 13. Sampur Dwima. 14. Call Centre. 15. Khapal Mwnda. 16. Khangkrai Officer Asi Bijou. 17. Jaounti Nerswn. 18. Malo Driver and 19. Bandh Culture.

2.3. From 2006 to 2008

Some other prominent books published in the year 2006 are "Kholta MLA Babu" by Jogendra Daimary, "Onnaini San" by Levenlal Mwchahary, "Raikos Fisa" by Uttara Bwiswmuthiary.

In the book "Raikos Fisa" by Uttara Bwiswmuthiary, there are eighteen (18) short stories. They are: 1. Adungari. 2. Mugani Daha. 3. Sanseni Habafari. 4. Khobai Lagra. 5. Rwimalini Haba. 6. Gaikherni Saha. 7. Pisajwnw Lirnai Laijam. 8. Alasi. 9. Onla arw Mwita. 10. Wngkham Jakhang nanwi rai janaibaidi. 11. Plasticni Gilas. 12. Saikhong. 13. Dwngse Khontai and 14. Daina. It has been published by Nijwm Khungur Bwiswmuthiary.

The book "Kitir" by Barua Kanta Brahma has been published in the year 2006. It has been published by Champawati Brahma. It consists of eight (8) stories. They are: 1. Birth Day. 2. Asi Rani mein mot Ana. 3. Oja Baila. 4. Jiuni Dwlwao Gwmanaini Saikongkou Gwswkangnanwi Dandise. 5. Alaisri. 6. Khiter and 7. Honglani Hangma.

The short story book by Swmkhwr is "Mwdwiyao Ma Dong". His original name is Gobindo Basumatary. It has been published in the year 2006. There are ten (10) short stories in this book. They are as follows: 1. Mwdwiyao Ma Dong. 2. Jwlwini Hangar. 3. Tirangtha Rwimalini. 4. Bwlw Khousetini. 5. Dukaru Sikouni Arojya Tarwi Sannai. 6. Montri. 7. Lwrbang Mijing. 8. Motonga Dwimani Mwdwi. 9 Simangni Kwika arw Mabwla Siri Mwnbaogwn.

Other short stories published in 2006 are as follows: "Alari" by Beremwdwi Mwchahary, "Phagunni Sansekali" by Dhanendra Brahma, "Fungkha" by Rabin Basumatary. It has been published by

Shamti Basumatary.

The book "Swima Bedor" by Bwhwisar Brahma has been published in the year 2006.

The book "Simang Na" by Shasikesh Basumatary has been published in the year 2006. It consists of five (5) short stories. They are as follows: 1. Girls Hostel. 2. Beha Megon Thaise. 3. Akai Mwnse Dongmwn. 4. Thik Thik Swr Dong. 5. Sijana and 6. Fwifinnai.

The book "Gwja Thwini Birlw" by Binita Uzir Basumatary has been published in the year 2006. It has been published by Biren Kumar Uzir.

The book "Hastainai" has been written by Mantri Brahma Chodhury in the year 2006. It has been published by Brahma Choudhury Publication.

The book "Bakundani Gwdan Formula" by Dhanuram Basumatary has been published in the year 2006. It has been published by Abindra Kumar Basumatary.

Some more books published in the year 2006 are "Fungkha" by Rabin Basumatary, "Hagra Juliyao Ombasi Hor" by Jogendra Basumatary and "Gwdan Okhafwr" by Binod Basumatary.

Some of the Bodo short story books published in the year 2007 are mentioned below:

The short story book "Gwrbwni Juliet Nagirnanwi" has been published by Oron Raja in the year 2007. There are sixteen (16) stories in this book which are as follows: 1. Orga Masterni Wngkham Gwrlwi. 2. Jinir. 3. Jwlao Lathiko. 4. Hor Gejerni Traged. 5. Maojini Adob. 6. Aluk. 7. Jilir. 8. Lathiko. 9. Gwrbwni Juliet Nagirnanwi. 10. Silingkar Saina Sali. 11. Junadni Kugayao Boro Thunlai. 12. Gwrbw Hojikraonai. 13. Bwdwr. 14. Neosijanai Bwrli. 15. Jilit Nangjabnai Daoharu and 16. Debwr.

The book "Manasni Thorse Hira" by Mithu Boro is a famous short story book. It has been published in the year 2007. There are ten (10) stories in this book which are as follows: 1. Angha Dongkhayw. 2. Garbwnai Bubli. 3. Manasni Thorse Hira. 4. Dahani Orgengjwng Deglaini Bwisagu. 5. Grotingso. 6. Durga Pujani Gudung Jilafi. 7. Busao Dandise. 8. Bordinni Pitha. 9. Feleng Radai.

10. Domasi Dinao Gwswm Rega.

The book “Bihamjw Hybrid” is the first book by Rabin Narzary. There are elephant (11) short stories in this book. It has been published in the year 2007. The stories in this book are as follows: 1. Jarou Sikwla. 2. Gwrwntiya Swrni. 3. Soithi Bimakou Mwntwngbw. 4. Daini. 5. Gongse Landang Canvavos. 6. Baiflenai Simang. 7. Gwbwrkini Mwikun. 8. Suspension. 9. Bihamjw Hybrid. 10. Ondla Rickshawala. 11. Sankhatiyanw Gwrwntisw.

The two books by Diganta Lahary are: 1. Mwdwijwng Lirnai Solo and 2. Bobe Lamajwng. It has been published by Nilima Prakashan in the year 2007.

The short story book “Hor Gejerni Polan” by Lebenlal Mushahary has been published in the year 2007. There are a total of twelve (12) short stories in this book. They are as follows: 1. Jwlwini Hangar Gwswya Gongse Mondir. 2. Subida Baidi AIDS. 3. Hor Gejerni Polan. 4. Gwswni Su. 5. Fungbili Tulungajwng. 6. Neosijanai Borad. 7. Bwisaguni Bokayao Mwkthang Bisombi. 8. Sinainw Mwnwi Oronni Bibar. 9. Kwmsi Okwrangni Rajalama and 10. Gwswya Mwnse Derhasar.

The book “Mwider Muhuni” by Janil Kumar Brahma has been published in the year 2007. There are twentysix (26) short stories in this book. They are as follows: 1. Kwila Jaonw Thangnai. 2. Retention Adhir. 3. Townni Bar. 4. Mwider Muhuni. 5. Orge. 6. Bijuli Baruah. 7. Oronni Daha. 8. Local Develop and others. It has been published by Dabari Basumatary.

The book “Daodab” written by Ranendra Swargiary is his first book. It has been published in the year 2007 by Chandra Ramchiary. There are nine (9) stories in this book. They are as follows - 1. Daodab. 2. Aluri. 3. Isaraya Jebla Jurani. 4. Ada Hongla. 5. Gab Gwywi Jaikhlong. 6. Solobayid Solo. 7. Afani Hatasuni and 8. Jwklwbnai Bijab.

The book “Gwdan Okhapwr” by Binod Basumatary is his first book. There are ten (10) short stories in this book. They are as follows: 1. Bibarni Mininai. 2. Gwdan Okhapwr. 3. Dimpaurao Ombasi. 4. Phanlu Bidwi. 5. Nameri. 6. Mwnse Gwswkhangjatao

Jathai. 7. Operation Sundaori. 8. Habruka Fami arw Jhumi. 9. The Gandhamadon expedition and 10. Gwmanai Dengkhw. It has been published by N.L. Publication in the year 2007.

The book "Ringni Ring" by Dhireswar Boro Narzary has been published in the year 2007 by N.L. Publication. There are 11 stories in this book.

The book "Sikri Sikla" by Subodh Gayary is a most remarkeable book. It has been published by Onsumai Library in the year 2007. There are twelve (12) short stories in this book. They are as follows: 1. Sikri Sikwla. 2. Fulmala. 3. Bombas Sanni Lis 4. Gwmwthao. 5. Mohima. 6. Bihari. 7. Maojiya. 8. Koro Gojo. 9. Ajwli Dera. 10. Horni Thandwi. 11. Simangni Solo and 12. Hor Gejerni Jathai.

The short story book "Daina" by Praneswar Boro has been published in the year 2007. There are twelve (12) short stories in this book.

Some more short stories published in the year 2007 are "Raja Rani" by Binoy Muchahary, "Professor Baneswar Mech" by Gopinath Brahma, "Hagrajuliyao Ombasi Hor" by Jogendra Daimary, "Bikaya Gaoyw Kugaya Geoya" by Firpila. It has been published by Swdwmshri Harimu Afad.

The book "SAronthai" by Oron Raja has been published by Bijni Boro Thunlai Afad. The book "88" by Okhafwr Laijwari has been published by Alendra Kumar Muchahary in the year 2007.

Some of the Bodo short stories published in the year 2008 are as follows:

The short story book "Gwrbw Khamglinai Or" by Lebenlal Muchahary has been published in the year 2008. It has been printed and published by Nilima Prakashan. There are ten (10) short stories in this book. They are as follows: 1. Offer Chowkidar. 2. Gwrwnti Nangou. 3. Gwrbw Khamglinai

Or. 4. Swima Lwikhwn. 5. Khiter. 6. Dukhu. 7. Phagunni Gangse Saogari. 8. Modernni Andwao and 9. Leader.

The book Sameli Rumbang" by Ronish Sangrang Ramchiary is a remarkeable one. It has been printed and published by Nilima Prakashan. There are fourteen (14) short stories in this book. They are as follows: 1. Sanwisw Gongwywi. 2. Ada Gwywi. 3. Julini Or. 4. Rajkhantiari Khaiser. 5. Meher Gwnang Dikar. 6. Sameli Rumbang. 7. Eselo Onnai. 8. Pocket Diary. 9. Cassete Dancesco. 10. Gwja Mwdwi. 11. Daola Berha. 12. Torse Sobai Bima. 13. Mohon Master and 14. Rojeni Fwrmainai Laijam.

The short story book “Daina” by Guneswar Muchahary has been published in the year 2008. There are sixteen (16) short stories in this book. This short story is related to witch.Some of the short stories in this book are: 1. Buhut. 2. Buhutni Saikhong. 3. Sikao arw Dukusrini Mwdwi and some others.

The book “Onjali Dhara” by Deobar Ramchiary has been published in the year 2008. There are ten (10) short stories in this book. They are: 1. Hafamuya. 2. Bibwnang Mela. 3. Dwikargra Mwdai. 4. Percentage. 5. Onjali Dhara. 6 Dwrwng. 7. Network. 8. Pen Friend. 9. Tornwi Hira. 10. Suburun and 11. Thulunga. It has been published by Nilima Prakashani.

The book “Lorhainai Gwrbwni Bibar” by Hainari Basumatary has been published in the year 2008 by Nilima Prakashani. It consists of twelve (12) short stories.

“Dodereni Hantase Jaiklong” is another short story by Hainari Basumatary. It has also been published by Nilima Prakashani in the year 2008.

The book “Jiu Lamayao Aganse” is the work of Barun Boro. It has been published in the year 2008 by Nilima Prakashani.

The short story “The Trap” is the work of Khuntiya Mushahary. There are twelve (12) short stories in this book.He is one of the best short story writer.

The book “Onthai Mwdai” by Birendra Kumar Basumatary is the second book by him. There are thirteen (13) short stories in this book. They are: 1. Sirinai Bibar. 2. Onthai Mwdai. 3. Asokanda Simang. 4. Hor Gejerni Sikwla. 5. Baleng. 6. Muli Rwda. 7. Sobita. 8. Arw Ang. 9. Gwrwnti ya Swrni. 10. Gwmw Katonta. 11. Nwng Haba Janw. 12. Najanaini Fithai. 13. Gwrwbnaini Dengkhw and 14. Nenaini Jwbtha Fithai.

The book "Bikhaya Gaoyw Kugaya Geoya" by Firpila Basumatary has been published in the year 2008. It has been published by Swdwmshri Harimu Afad.

"A Collection of Bodo Short Stories" by Bodo Publication Board has been published in the year 2008.

The short story book "Solo Bihung" is a valuable book which has been published by Bodo Sahitya Sabha. There are fiftyseven (57) short stories in this book. It has been published in the year 2008.

The book "Jiu Dwimani Guthal" is the first book by Rwirup Brahma. There are thirteen (13) short stories in this book. They are: 1. Okafwrni Dagwao Gwswm Dagw. 2. Gwrwntiya Nwngnilo Nonga. 3. Ganw Rwngwi Berai. 4. Jiuni Lamayao. 5. Undaha. 6. Greetings Card. 7. Bwisagu Rongjanw Gamiyao Tangni Tou. 8. Bwisaguni Sanjoufu Bubliyao. 9. Habani Astham. 10. Bwiswni Dengkhw. 11. Jiu Dwimani Guthal. 12. Gwrwntini Bibar and 13. Nwjwrni Hangma.

The book "Gwjanni Solo Subungni Solo" by Gobindo Basumatary has been published in the year 2008. There are eight (8) short stories in this book.

The book "Sanjoufu Barhungka" by Dhiren Boro is his first short story book. It has been published in the year 2008.

The book "Haoasi" by Uttara Bwiswmuthiary is one of the remarkeable book.It has been published by Nijwm Khungur Bwiswmuthiary.

2.4. From 2009 to 2010

Some of the Bodo short stories published in the year 2009 are as follows:

The short story book "Onnaini Sao" by Lebenlal Mwchahary consists of elephant (11) short stories. Another important book by him is "Red Signal".

Both these books has been published in the year 2009 by Nilima Prakashani.

In the short story book "Red Signal" there are elephant (11) short stories. They are as follows: 1. Dwijlang. 2. Onnaini San. 3. Fandaisuli Sonima. 4. Daosin Haba. 5. Onnaini Munga Mwnish

Gwdwi. 6. Miss Barma College. 7. Gidir Mansi. 8. Simang Dandali. 9. Gongse Dwima: Tonggwiyi Gongtam Dinga. 10. Gwrbw Fwisaliyao Onamika. 11. Man.

The short stories in the book "Onnaini Sao" are as follows: 1. Simangni Rwbwi Mijingni Fwisali. 2. Red Signal. 3. Khouse Agan. 4. Sayafwra Ang. 5. Jwngha Gederfwrabw Lecture Hwjayw. 6. Dinwini Subung. 7. Jwngha Biban Dong. 8. Sanjaha Alaiaron: Swnabha Mwnabili. 9. Sungdo Soloni Nagirnanwi. 10. Cross Connection.

The short story book "Japanni Swima" by Janil Kumar Brahma is an important book. This book has been published in the year 2009. It has been published by Bodo Publication Board. There are twenty (20) short stories in this book. They are as follows: 1. Orge. 2. Dao Kela. 3. Honglemwnniyao Bilifangni Party. 4. Dabaoswi Fwigwn Bwisagwyao. 5. Daosrigwba. 6. Japanni Swima. 7. Khwmsi Golini Andwyao. 8. Gomta Masterni Kapal. 9. Kamblao Mahajwnni Blood Pressure. 10. Kawang. 11. Malaria. 12. Terlani Simang. 13. Dabla Garifani Songsar. 14. Montri Fwigwn. 15. Hajwni Sikiri Hayenni Bibar. 16. Megon Doctor. 17. Sonani Medal. 18. Kwilashpurni Motham Mahajwn. 19. Training. 20. Lama Seraoni Taso Bibar.

The book "Mwdwi" by Rajen Basumatary is an important book. It is the second book by him. It has been published by Habari Basumatary. There are nine (9) short stories in this book. They are as follows: 1. Kwirwm Dwirwm. 2. Mwdwi. 3. Compromise. 4. Adhyotiliyao Juli. 5. Bwijad. 6. Meonaijwngki Hayw. 7. Rimikos Lamani Bibar and 8. Modirani Thwi.

The book "Beduin" by Sahitya Akademi Awardee Jwishri Boro is a remarkeable one. It has been published in the year 2009. There are ten (10) short stories in this book. They are as follows: 1. Professor Laheram. 2. Maoriya. 3. Alayaron. 4. Jiu Saharani Beduin. 5. Bihamjw Mongli. 6. Hangma Hangsani Agor Fali. 7. Propjyal. 8. Honglani Songsar. 9. Fwthaikebso and 10. Subha. It has been published by Nilima Prakashani.

The book "Mekong Dwimani Laijam" by Umesh Brahma is his first book. There are sixteen (16) short stories in this book. They are as follows: 1. Sinaijaywi Junad. 2. Okafwrni Mwdwi. 3. Doumo.

4. Swimanifrai Sangrang Jaa. 5. Swnabni Bar. 6. Repeater. 7. Beohai Dwima Gwiyabla Hamgoumwn. 8. Simangna Mwkthang. 9. Sase Gwmwthao Spy Hinjao. 10. Mengko Dwimani Laijam. 11. Arabian Ferenga Dao. 12. Post Mortem. 13. Statement. 14. Mwnabilini Swdwmshri. 15. La Bele Dai Sense Marcy. 16. Ww and 17. Epaje Dwimani Gisikanai Habrang.

The book "Jarou Polan" is the creation of Samar Narzary. It has been published in the year 2009.

The book "Nangalni Mwdwikou Hugargwn Swr" by Sunil Kumar Boro is one of his remarkable book.There are fourteen (14) short stories in this book. They are as follows: 1. Asokanda. 2. Julini Sanao Onthwb. 3. Jiraitonal Subungni Jiu. 4. Jorase Sadrwi Soka Dao. 5. Nangalni Mwdwikou Hugargwn Swr. 6. Tailali Masterni Borai. 7. Nwrmoholni Lorhailangnai Barse Bibar. 8. Matham Mwdaijw. 9. Magwni or Sapnai Bwrwi. 10. Garbwnai Lamathing. 11. Houyani Raga Bisini Fao. 12. Simangni Manik. 13. Bangalni Khapalao Gwja Sindur and 14. Lwrbangtini Fithai.

The short story book "Kasim Ali Hindu Hotel" by Rwisumwi (Dhajen Swargiary) is a remarkeable book. There are twentyfive (25) short stories in this book. They are as follows: 1. Tender Notice: Bijamadwi Nangou. 2. Deglai Nonga Khalmasisw. 3. Beoyaifwr Sanjarwi Jiu Bendwng. 4. Pwipinbaobai Dwimaluya. 5. Be Haya Jwngni. 6. Half Sufetar. 7. Gwmwrnai Sindur. 8. Election. 9. Mwnnai Mwnwi Fallini Munga Romfabati. 10. Beauty Queen. 11. Kwinasanthi. 12. Golai Gujai. 13. Istahar. 14. Hangkur. 15. Nwlw Hagrani Jagra. 16. Dogo Mogo

The book "Gwrwntiya Swrnimwn" by Rupmal Boro has been published in the year 2010. There are eighteen (18) stories in this book. They are as follows: 1. Khwmsi Singsar. 2. Alasi. 3. Gwjam Diaryni Saogir. 4. Dahani Mwdwi. 5. Mwnse Saogir. 6. Julini Somai. 7. Saikhong. 8. Beram. 9. Mwnabili Dengkhw. 10. Gwrwntiya Swrnimwn Orong. 11. Greetings. 12. Gwrwnti Dwimal Mijing. 13. Gwrbwni Mwdwi. 14. Jethw. 15. Lama Nainw and 16. Gwjam Onjalu.

The book “Thamjinwi Musuka Solo Batha” b Pramila Narzary has been published in the year 2010. There are thirtyfour (34) short stories in this book.

The short story book “Phanjarini Dao” by Subodh Gayary has been published in the year 2010 by Onsumwi Library.

The book “Hawasi” by Promod Kumar Brahma has been published in the year 2010 by Onsumwi Library.

There are nine (9) short stories in this book. They are: 1. Bibiyai Dorson. 2. Phanjari. 3. Gang Gwnang Sila. 4. Ating Mongolni Wngkham. 5. Jaoliya Dewanni Akuthai. 6. Ramanda Masterni Bethon. 7. Gwmanai Painting. 8. Jolonggani Pitha and 9. Habasi.

The book “Trainya Kargolangbai” by Rekha Basumatary has been published in the year 2010. There are ten (10) short stories in this book. They are: 1. Budelni Gathwnao. 2. Sithaoya Khambai. 3. Trainya Kargolangbai. 4. Rojeni Laijam. 5. Abou Rantheng. 6. Jwnghani Langwnayao Swrniba Thopola. 7. Lamani Thorse Onthai. 8. Onnaikou Swrnw Hwbaonw. 9. Megonayao Maniba Mwdwi. 10. Doorya Geonai Nongamwnbwla.

The book “Bon Gami Hagra Gamini 1989 maithaini swima sikari” by Samar Narzary has been published in the year 2010.

The book “Toflase Sungdo Solo” edoted by Gopinath Brahma has been published in the year 2010. There are twenty (20) short stories in this book.

The book “Original Carbon Copy” by Khameswar Boro has been published in the year 2010. It has been published by Priyasa Boro.

The book “Jolonga” by Ramani Bilas Mwchahary has been published in the year 2010.

The book “Mwnnwi Mwkhang Gwbang Mohor” by Dr. Sunil Pukhan Basumatary has been published in the year 2010. It has been published by Onsumwi Library. The short story book “Delhini Lahu” by Nila Hainary has been published in the year 2010.

Some other books published in the year 2010 are “Pothou Sanwini Solo” by Purna Kanta Basumatary, “Nangalni Mwdwikou Hugargwn Swr” by Nilima Boro, Kochari Pwrwnggirini Habilas by Pursu Ramchiary.

The book "Simang Mwkthang" by Birphung Narzary and Raju Narzary has been published by Narzary Brothers in the year 2010.

The book "Solo Bihung" by Boro Sahitya Sabha has been published in the year 2010. There are sixty-six (66) short stories in this book.

It has been noticed that the number of short stories in Bodo literature has been increasing more in the period from 2000 to 2010.

3.0. Conclusion

In the short stories, the story writer used to modern technique and new theme. It has been making the new idea, used of technology, and depended on the economic development. There are many short stories influenced on the modern perspective. So, the Bodo short story are very widely growth and development in this ten years.

References

1. Basumatary Bijitgiri - Nwjwr Arw Sanshri (A Pross Collection), 2009 Second edition. Onsumai library, Kokrajhar Assam)
2. Basumatary Dr. Bijitgiri – Society and culture on Bodo short stories. 1st edition Mrs. Hiramuni Basumatary, Chirang B.T.A.D. (Assam)
3. Basumatary, Rakhao – Thunlai Bijirnai (Criticism of Boro literature) 1994. Bodo Publication Boor, Bodo Sahitya Sobha, Kokrajhar, (Assam)
4. Basumatary, Rakhao –Boro Sungdo Soloni Jarinim, 2nd edition, 2013 words & word, Kokrajhar Bodoland India.
5. Basumatary Dr. Adaram – Nwiji Jouthaini Thunlai Bijirnai, 1st edition, 2019. Onsumai library, R.N.B. Road, Kokrajhar
6. Basumatary Z.D. – Mister Hybridni Gwlwmdwi Arw Mwdwi, (Short Story), 1st edition, February, 2005, Chirang Publication Board, Dhaligaon.
7. Boro Madhuram – Jariminni nwjwrao Boro Thunlai (History of Boro literature), 1998 Priyadini Publications Hajo, Kamrup (Assam)

8. Boro Jwishree – Jiu Saharani Beduin. 1st edition, 2015, Words & Words, RNB Road, Kokrajhar, Bodoland
9. Brahma Brajendra Kr. – Thunlai arw Shanshri (Prose collection), 1998 onsumai library, kokrajhar, (Assam)
10. Brahma Haribhusan – Shrimuthi Durlai, 198, W.L. Publication, Kokrajhar (Assam)
11. Brahma, Janil Kumar; Dumphaoni Pitha (2005); Onsumwi Library, RNB Road, Kokrajhar, BTR Assam.
12. Brahma, Janil Kumar, Japanni Swima, 2nd edition, 2017, Bodo Publication Board, Bodo Sahitya Sabha.
13. Brahma Nil Kamal – Hagra Guduni Mwi (Deer of the Virgin Forest). 1972, Onsumai library, Kokrajhar (Assam)
14. Brahma Nilkamal – Sakandra (Kidnaper) 1987 onsumai library, Kokrajhar (Assam)
15. Brahma Nilkamal – Silingkhar (Destruction) 1984, Bodo publication Board, Bodo sahitya Sobha, Kokrajhar (Assam)
16. Brahma Nilkamal – Sirinai Mander Bibar (Falten Monder Flower). 1985, Sijou publication Board, Bijni Chirang (Assam)
17. Brahma Riju Kr. – Boro Thunlaini Jarimin arw Thunlai Bijirnai (A History & a criticism of Bodo Literature) 2nd edition, 2007, onsumai library, RNB Road Kokrajhar, Bodoland.
18. Lahary Monoranjan – History of Boro literature. 3rd edition, 2008, Onsumai library, Kokrajhar, B.T.A.D. Assam.
19. Mushahary Chittaranjan – Phwimal Mijing (Spolied Imagination) 1990, Publication KOkrajhar (Assam).
20. Swargiary Kathindra - Hangla Pandit, 1995 Kitap Samalya, Punbazar, Guwahati - I. Assam.

English Book Section

1. David Lodge & Nigel Wood (Edited), Modern Criticism and Theory, 2004 2nd edition, Person Education (Singapore) pte.Ltd. India Branch, 482 F.I.E. Patparagoni, Delhi 110092 India.
2. Gait Sir Edward, A History of Assam. 1st edition, 1905, Bina library, College Hostel Road, Panbazar, Guwahati – 781001,

Assam

3. Kakati Dr. B.K.- Assamese: Its Formation and Development.
4. Nath Rajmohan – Background of Assamese culture
5. Sen Dr. Sukumar: On Bodo language.
6. Waugh Patrica, Literary Theory and criticism, 2006, 1st Edition, OXFORD University Press, YMCA Library Building, Jaising Road New D*elhi 11001.*

CHAPTER FIVE

A STUDY ON POLITITICAL VIEW OF THE SHORT STORY 'MONTRI FWIGWN'

Abstract

In the discussion, in the Short Story 'Montri Pwigwn' (A Minister will Come) by Janil Kumar Brahma is a short story which is based on political in nature. The story is based on a village in which a minister will be visiting before election. The short story was published in the year 2009. Most of the people in the village were leading poor lives. Their living style were backward. For that reason, the villagers were making a great celebration during the time of the Rongjali Bwisagu festival. The village headmen was organizing the festival with great enthusiasm and he also announced before the villagers that a minister will be visiting their village. The Minister was on his way to election campaign where he will be convincing the villagers to caste their votes in favour of him. The poor villagers were so much influenced by the sweet words of the Minister and MLA. Apart from that, the village leaders without caring for their families also rund after the Minister. Such types of political sceneario is seen before each and every election now-a-days. After election, the Minister never comes to visit the village again. It has been reflected through this short story. As we all know that most of the Ministers and MLAs used to make false promises during the time of the elections. In this way, most of the villagers are convinced by the politicians during the time of the elections.

Keywords : Political, Village People and Bodo Culture

1.0. Introduction

The Short Story 'Montri Pwigwn' (A Minister will Come) by Janil Kumar Brahma is a short story which is political in nature. The story is based on a village in which minister will be visiting. Most of the people in the village were leading poor lives. Their living style were backward. For that reason, the villagers were making a great celebration during the time of the Rongjali Bwisagu festival. The village headmen was organizing the festival with great enthusiasm and he also announced before the villagers that a minister will be visiting their village. The Minister named Tublao Brahma also informed that he will be positively visiting the village through urgent telegram.

The Minister was on his way to election campaign where he will be convincing the villagers to caste their votes in favour of him. The Minister has stated, "Father, Mother, and my dear Bodo sons and daughters. I have come to visit your village. Election is coming. Please don't forget to vote for me. If I become minister once again, I will provide you various opportunities like schools, colleges, roads, bridges and so on. You keep in mind that if I become Minister once again, your village will become like a heaven.

The poor villagers were so much influenced by the sweet words of the Minister and MLA. Apart from that, the village leaders without caring for their families also rund after the Minister.

Such types of political sceneario is seen before each and every election now-a-days. After election, the Minister never comes to visit the village again. It has been reflected through this short story. As we all know that most of the Ministers and MLAs used to make false promises during the time of the elections. In this way, most of the villagers are convinced by the politicians during the time of the elections.

Just like the village Headmen, when he along with his family went to caste their vote together during the elections, the theif has entered their house taking advantage of the situation since there was none in their home. The thief has looted all their belongings.

Apart from that, most of the poor villagers also used to get together during the time of the elections if an MLA or a Minister uses to visit their village. For that reason, the villagers of the Moamari village also used to gather to meet the Minister. From this viewpoint, we can see that how the Ministers or the MLAs use to make false promises to the villagers.

Most of the politicians use to make false promises to the villagers by asking them to vote in favour of him like the ministers will be stating that they will be providing them with various opportunities like schools, colleges, roads, bridges and so on.

We have also seen that some MLAs and Ministers use to purchase the voters by using money.

Some of the village level also feels themselves to be of respectable person by campaigning along with the Ministers. Just like the village headman, who was travelling in the car along with the DSP and Minister felt himself like a great leader. The village headman has also forgotten the daily needs of his family by travelling along with the politician.

Such types of scene are very common these days, where the village people use to forget their basic needs by being mislead by the politicians. These incidents are very common now-a-days, especially during the time of elections. We have seen that the politicians use to convince the villagers by making false promises.

1.2. Aim and Objectives

The aims and objectives of the short story are as follows:

(i) Political

(ii) Village People

(iii) Bodo Culture.

The main aims and objectives of this paper is to discuss the above mentioned topics.

1.3. Methodology

In this short story, analytical method has been used. Various types of data has been collected. Both primary as well as secondary data has been collected. For primary data, questionnaire method has been used and for secondary data, it has been collected from various textbooks.

1.4. Review of Literature

In this discussion, some of the books written on literature has been taken as a reference. One of them is the book 'Boro Sungdo Soloni Jarimin' (A History of Bodo Short Stories) by Rakhao Basumatary. The other book is Jipanni Swima by Janil Kumar Brahma. One more prominent book is the book 'Modern Literary Theory' by Rice Philip and Waugh Patricia.

2. 0.Political

The Short Story 'Montri Pwigwn' (A Minister will Come) by Janil Kumar Brahma is a short story which is political in nature. The story is based on a village in which minister will be visiting. Most of the people in the village were leading poor lives. Their living style were backward. For that reason, the villagers were making a great celebration during the time of the Rongjali Bwisagu festival. The village headmen was organizing the festival with great enthusiasm and he also announced before the villagers that a minister will be visiting their village. The Minister named Tublao Brahma also informed that he will be positively visiting the village through urgent telegram.

The Minister was on his way to election campaign where he will be convincing the villagers to caste their votes in favour of him. The Minister has stated, "Father, Mother, and my dear Bodo sons and daughters. I have come to visit your village. Election is coming. Please don't forget to vote for me. If I become minister once again, I will provide you various opportunities like schools, colleges, roads, bridges and so on. You keep in mind that if I become Minister once again, your village will become like a heaven.

The poor villagers were so much influenced by the sweet words of the Minister and MLA. Apart from that, the village leaders without caring for their families also rund after the Minister.

Such types of political scenario is seen before each and every election now-a-days. After election, the Minister never comes to visit the village again. It has been reflected through this short story. As we all know that most of the Ministers and MLAs used to make false promises during the time of the elections. In this way, most of the villagers are convinced by the politicians during the time of the elections.

Just like the village Headmen, when he along with his family went to caste their vote together during the elections, the thief has entered their house taking advantage of the situation since there was none in their home. The thief has looted all their belongings.

Apart from that, most of the poor villagers also used to get together during the time of the elections if an MLA or a Minister uses to visit their village. For that reason, the villagers of the Moamari village also used to gather to meet the Minister. From this viewpoint, we can see that how the Ministers or the MLAs use to make false promises to the villagers.

Most of the politicians use to make false promises to the villagers by asking them to vote in favour of him like the ministers will be stating that they will be providing them with various opportunities like schools, colleges, roads, bridges and so on.

We have also seen that some MLAs and Ministers use to purchase the voters by using money.

Some of the village level also feels themselves to be of respectable person by campaigning along with the Ministers. Just like the village headman, who was travelling in the car along with the DSP and Minister felt himself like a great leader. The village headman has also forgotten the daily needs of his family by travelling along with the politician.

Such types of scene are very common these days, where the village people use to forget their basic needs by being mislead by the politicians. These incidents are very common now-a-days, especially during the time of elections. We have seen that the politicians use to convince the villagers by making false promises.

3.0. Village people

We have seen that most of the people of Moamari village are village people and illiterate people where their living style is backward like lack of education, poor life style and so on. It has been reflected in the short story "Montri Pwigwn (A Minister will Come)". Here in this short story, at least two major topics have been highlighted like :

(i) Village People and

(ii) Illiterate Village People.

(i) The poor villagers are very eager to meet the Ministers. In the same way, one day the villagers are going to organize a Bwisagu festival. Most of the villagers were taking part in the meeting since they already heard the news that a minister will be visiting their village.Then the wife of the village headman asked her husband, "Why are you asking the villagers to attend the programme of such a minister who comes to visit the village only once in 12 years?'' You much not do that. I will see what he is going to say.Then the daughter of the village headman replied, "Daddy, whatever you said is not good. As the villagers are preparing to celebrate the Bwisagu, we can't have the Minister's programme. Then the maid servant of the Village Headman said, "I have also not seen a Minister; whether he is a man or a God. I wanted to see the Minister." From the above statement, we can understand two terms, that some of the village people knows the dirty politics of the minister while others are uneducated people.

(ii) Illiterate Village people

In each and every village, we can find lots of uneducated people. Only a few educated people can be found in most of the villages. In the same way, most of the people of Moamari village also use to worship their village headman as their leader. For that reason, the village headman of the Moamari village has been invited in each and every meetings of the village.

Almost all the uneducated people use to follow the orders of the village headman.

Then the village headman said to his wife, "Tomorrow, as you all know that there will be a minister programme. So only I can lead the programme and in my absence the programme is going to get cancelled. So, it will be good if you can stay at home in the absence of me. He also said that there are petty thefts in the village who use to steal small items including utensils. So, it will be better for you not to attend the minister programme and stay at home." From the above statement, we come to know that the village headman is not wanting his wife and family members to attend the minister programme.

Moreover, the village headman also stated to his daughter Bangbuli, "My daughter Bangbuli, You please don't go to the meeting since you are an unmarried young girl. I will buy a golden necklace for you. Please stay at home." He also asked his maid servant, "You need not go to the meeting tomorrow, rather you please take care of home. I will give you a reward. You don't need to see the minister as he is also a human being, but not a God." The Village Headman want any one of his family member to stay at home. But he is not able to convince anyone. Finally, he has to leaved everyone go to the meeting.

4.0. The Bodo Culture

Culture is like the mirror of a community. Just like whatever is there in our face is reflected in a mirror, in the same way, each and every community is reflected with the help of their culture. In the short story "Montri Pwigwn" by Janil Kumar Brahma, some of the cultures of Bodo community has been reflected.

From the words of the village headman, some of the traditional knowledge of the Bodo women have been reflected, "Bodo women can beautifully weave their traditional attires. With the help of the beautiful traditional attire Aronai, which has been weaved by the Bodo women, we can welcome our Minister."Apart from that, they can also perform their beautiful traditional dance with the help of their musical instruments. They are also active in their works and making traditional beverage like wine. They use to worship their traditional festivals with great enthusiasm. From the above statement, some of the cultures, customs and traditions of the Bodo society has been reflected.

5.0. Conclusion

From the above discussion, it can find the short story "Montri Pwigwn (A Minister will Come) by Janil Kumar Brahma is political in nature. It has also reflected the village people, uneducated people and Bodo culture. The story has some relation to Bodo culture. It has reflected the traditional knowledge of Bodo women like weaving traditional attires and traditional dances performed by Bodo women. It has also reflected some of the common scenes before elections, which are seen now a days like a Minister visiting a village and making fake promises. People use to forget their daily needs of the family by campaigning along with the Minister where sometimes even thieves enter their houses taking advantage of no one at home when people usually goes out to vote. All these scenes have been reflected in this short story.

References :

1. Basumatary, Rakhao : A History of Bodo short Stories, Words & Words , 2nd Edition, 2013 Kokrajhar, Bodoland, India.Brahma, Janil Kumar : Japanni Swima, Bodo Publication Bord, 2nd Edition, 2017, Bodo Sahitya Sabha.
2. Rice Philip & Waugh Patricia (Edited) : Modern Literary Theory, Distributed in the United states of America by Oxford University Press Enc. 198 Modison Avenue, New York, NY 10016, Fourth Edition, 2001.
3. Waugh Patricia, Literary Theory and Criticism, 2006 1st Edition. Oxford University Press. YMCA Library Building, Jaising Road, New Delhi 11001.

CHAPTER SIX

The Reflection of Political View in the Short Story 'Open Session' Abstract

Abstract

The short story Geolang Mel (Open Session) is a part of the book Mr. Hybrid Gwlwmdwi arw Mwdwi by J.D. Basumatary. The book has been published in February 2005. There are thirty short stories in this book. The book is mainly based on the political scenario of Bodoland Movement. In this short story, we can find that after achieving Bodoland, different communities living in Bodoland are demanding for the promotion and protection of their rights like preservation of language, culture, identity and so on. It has also been discussed that whether people are really satisfied with Bodoland or not. It has also been discussed that people from different communities are willing to live together in Bodoland. So, we can find that political scenario is reflected in the short story Geolang Mel.

Keywords : Political, Leader, Indigenous People.

1.1. Introduction

The short story Geolang Mel (Open Session) is a remarkable creation by J.D. Basumatary. The short story is included in the book "Mr. Hybrid: Gwlwmdwi arw Medwi" which won Sameswari Thunlaiari Vantha (Sameswari Literary Award) in the year

2006.The short story Geolang Mel (Open Session) is mainly based on political scenario. In the short story, the political scenario of the Bodos like Bodoland Movement and the demand for an independent nation as well as the clashes between the Bodos and the non-Bodos has been reflected. The leaders of different Bodo organizations who jointly led the Bodoland Movement has also been reflected in the short story. In this short story, some of the demands of the non-Bodos like protection of their identify and culture as well as religion after the Bodoland Accord has also been reflected.

The story began with the open session in the annual mass gathering of different Bodo organizations at a field named Boro's Utumai Khongkor Jahar.

It ended with the President's speech at the end of the program.

In this short story, apart from organizing the programme, it has also been reflected that the President of the organizing committee Gwlwndang Brahma has also welcomed the invited as well as uninvited guest with the traditional Aronai. Some of the organizations of the open session, which has been reflected in the short story are Dularai Boro Poraisha Afad, Dularai Boro Aijw Ansuli Afad, Dularai Boro Thunlaishrwn Afad, Dhularai Boro Shakor Afad, Dularai Boro Rwnaoshrwn Afad, Dularai Boro Halouswm Afad and Dularai Boro Rebshrwn Afad. The mass gathering has been jointly organized by seven different organizations. It has been organised for seven days. Some of the political scenario has also been reflected in the short story like the leaders of the different organizations has delivered lectures and stated that after achieving Bodoland, all the indigenous communities must live together in peace and harmony.

1.2. Objectives of the study

The aims of the discussion are as follows :

(I) To discuss about political scenario.

(II) To discuss about leading organizations.

(III) To discuss about indigenous communities.

1.3. Research Methodology

In this discuss, analytical method has been used. Both primary as well as secondary data has been collected. For primary data, primary level books and for secondary data, reference books has been collected.

1.4. Literature Review

In this discussion, some books has been collected as a reference. Some of them are as follows: Boro Sungdo Soloni Jarimin (History of Bodo Short Stories) by Rakhao Basumatary, Mister Hybrid: Gelwmdwi arw Mwdwi by J.D. Basumatary, Boro Sungdo Soloni Dahar by Swarna Prabha Chainary. These are some of the books, which have been taken as a reference.

1.5. Importance

The main significance of this discussion is that some of the political scenario of the Bodoland Movement has been reflected like after achieving a separate state of Bodoland, all the indigenous communities must live together in unity, peace and harmony as stated by the leaders of the different organizations.

2.1. Political

From this scenario, we have come to know that all people are not satisfied and are demanding more rights. After that, the President of the Bwrlashrwn Afad, Birsa Marandi has stated that, "We also wanted to live in Bodoland together along with the Bodos. But the Bodo people must also respect our cultures like rat and hare hunting and taking bows and arrows. Otherwise we are also ready to use our bows and arrows."

The President of the Dari Gwlao Afad, Muhammad Abduz Mannan Shiekh, "We also want to live together in Bodoland along with the Bodos in peace and harmony. But the Bodos must also respect our rights like taking additional wives, taking beard, wearing lungi and tufi and so on. Otherwise, we will also be taking long bamboo sticks. The President of the Hangsw Afad, Songram Singha has stated that, "We also wanted to live in Bodoland forever." But the Bodoland government must respect our rights like drying Chira and Muris. Otherwise we will be compelled to take up arms. The President of the Embushrwn Afad, Debashish Ghosh has stated that we like frogs also want to lay eggs everywhere be it rivers, lakers Or ponds and increase our future generations. Otherwise we will also be compelled to take up arms. From the above discussion, we have come to know about the political scenario.

3.1. Leaders

In the short story Geolang Mel (Open Session), the writer has stated about the situations, which usually takes place during an open session. In the open session, seven different organizations took part to discuss different issues after achieving Bodoland. In the open session, we have seen that the different organizations have been putting up different demands. In the open session, different organizations along with the public have taken part. The meeting has been organized for one week. People have been participating in the meeting in the hope of getting some good news. People from various communities have been coming to take part in the meeting.

The people from different organizations like President Nara Bahadur Chetry, President of the Bwrlashrwn Afad, Birsa Marandi, President of the Dari Gwlao Afad, Muhammad Abduz Mannan Shiekh, President of the Hangsw Afad, Songram Singha and President of the Embushrwn Afad, Debashish Ghosh.

In the open session different people have been invited who took part in the Bodoland Movement from 1987-2003. Apart from that, many uninvited people also took part in the open session. Different quotas have been kept for different people like separate quotas for Bodoland Movement martyr's families and so on. People from different communities have also been putting up their different demands in the meeting.

In the open session, the meeting was presided over by Gwlwndang Brahma. After that, the introduction of guests was done by convenor Rankw. The guests are welcomed with the traditional attire Aronai. After one hour, four bundles of Aronai were given to the people. But still some of the people have not got the Aronai including a sitting MLA. Then the President of the organising committee Gwlwndang Brahma has ordered, "Go and bring more Aronai. Hurry up!" After that, the volunteers were in a hurry to bring more Aronai.

4.1. Indigenous People

In the short story Geolang Mel, it has been reflected that different people have been demanding their rights after achieving Bodoland like promotion and protection of their culture, customs, language, traditions and so on. People from various communities have been coming to take part in the meeting. The people from different organizations like President Nara Bahadur Chetry, President of the Bwrlashrwn Afad, Birsa Marandi, President of the Dari Gwlao Afad, Muhammad Abduz Mannan Shiekh, President of the Hangsw Afad, Songram Singha and President of the Embushrwn Afad, Debashish Ghosh. Apart from that, the writer has also mentioned about the kind and peace loving nature of the Bodos.

5.0. Conclusion

In the conclusion, finally we can find the reflections of the agitating Bodos and the demands of the non-Bodos rights in the short story Geolang Mel. So, we can say that the political scenario of Bodoland has been reflected in this short story. In the short story Geolang Mel, it has been reflected that different people have been demanding their rights after achieving Bodoland like promotion and protection of their culture, customs, language, traditions and so on. From this scenario, we have come to know that all people are not satisfied and are demanding more rights.

References :

1. Basumatary, Z.D. : Mistar Hybridni Gwlwmdwi arw Mwdwi, Chirang Publication Bord, Dhaligaon, Chirang, First Edition, 2005.
2. Basumatary, Rakhao : Boro Sungdo Soloni Jarimin, Words & Words, Kokrajhar, Bodoland, India, Second Edition, 2013.
3. Chainary, Swarna Prabha : Boro Sungdo Soloni Bwhwithi Dahar (Edited), Sahitya Akademi, Bodo Depertment, Gauhati University, Second Edition, 2014.

CHAPTER SEVEN

People living near the 'Ujani Dongo' River and the fearful incidents in their daily lives : A Discussion

Abstract

The Short Story 'Gonggar Hajwni Dwi' (Water of Gongar Hill) is one of the remarkable short story by Z.D. Basumatary. The short story is included or can be found in the book "Mr. Hybrid: Gwlwmdwi arw Mwdwi". There are a total of 30 short stories in this book. The book has won Sameswari Literary Award in the year 2006. It is his book published for the second time. His first published book was entitled 'Ang Fwifingwn'. He is a remarkable short story writer.

1.1. Introduction

In this part, the researcher used to give a brief description on the short story 'Gongar Hajwni Dwi'. The short story begun in the month of Ashar from 10 PM in the midnight till morning. The central theme of this story is based on a river named 'Ujani Dongo' which is located near the house of Nirmala and Khungkhra who are wife and husband in relation respectively and their daughter Roje. In the story, it has been mentioned that black clouds are flying and floating from East to West in the sky. Sometimes it is also lightning. The lighting are like long lights blinking. May be it's going to rain shortly. The rain may continue non-stop. It's like a season. Just like each and everything is active during it's season. May be it may even leas to floods. Nirmali has been waiting for her husband. He has left few moments ago, but still not returned home yet. He has went to meet the Executive Engineer of an Irrigation Department and was trying to have lunch.

At that time, their telephone used to rung in a kring kring kring kring tune in the night time.

Nirmali is little afraid whether it was her husband or another evil person. Her daughter Raje was already asleep. The anyways Nirmali used to pick up the receiver.

Hello

Is it you, Mom.

Yes. How many bottles left.

Still One and half left. But I think time is up.

What time is up. It's just 10 PM now. Still six hours left for the next morning.

Are you teasing me? If I tell you the truth you will be afraid.

What is that truth? Please tell me.

No no. It's just a joke. Iam going home. Right now I'm on the way. Have you had your dinner.

I haven't taken yet. Iam waiting for you.

Its OK. Its OK. You should not be convinced like Sita. Please tell what curry you have prepared.

There is no good curry. Its just snail and sour and dal.

The Bhutanese people are releasing water from the hills. I have heard it. In the plains, the water may come up to 7 to 8 feet and may wash and destroy all our properties in the night. It may reach our village by 2:30 PM. Others have already prepared to deal with the situation. So let's pack our belongings like clothes, food and money. I have made a canoe by cutting one of our banana plant.

Are you joking or what by drinking. Who told you?

Iam Madan from Barpeta Bwrsijora. In our side, the flood flowing from Bhutan Hills have created havoc in the areas lying near the Beki river. In your Aie River side, isn't there flood.

The flood will flow towards our side by 2:30. Just now, we have packed our belongings.

So we are busy now. Let's talk another day.

What shall we do Dad? Our Madan has said that the Beki river has created havoc. What shall we do now? Where shall we go now?

In this story, we have seen that Khungra and Nirmali had a discussion on lightning, flood washing away the properties, packing up their belongings and so on.

1.2. Aim of the Study

The aim of discussion in this short story are as follows :

I. A Discussion on Indigenous People
II. A Discussion on Ujani Dongo
III. A Discussion on Challenges
IV. A Discussion on Traditional Curry.

1.3. Methodology

The Methods used in this study are based on literature review and analytical method. Because it's a easy method of discussion. It can be expressed easily. The Collection is based on both Primary and Secondary Data. In primary data, textbook has been used and in secondary data, discussion has been adopted.

1.5. Literary Discussion

In this discussion, some books as reference has been adopted. Some of these books are Boro Sungdo Soloni Jarimin (History of Bodo short stories) by Rakhao Basumatary, Mr. Hybrid: Gwlwmdwi arw Mwdwi by JD Basumatary and Sujunai Boro Sungdo Soloni Bwhwiti Dahar by Swarna Prabha ChainaryChainary.

1.6. Importance

The importance of this discussion is based on the Indigenous People living near the Ujani Dongo river and the situation they face during floods.

2.1. Indigenous People

In the story Gongar Hajwni Dwi, it has been discussed about the Indigenous People who are living near the rivers flowing from Bhutan Hills like Ujani Dongo. In this story, the lives of the Indigenous People has been reflected like food habits, agriculture, lifestyle, traditional curry and so on. We have seen that the Indigenous People use to make their own requirements with the help of Traditional Knowledge. In the short story, the lives of the Indigenous People living near the Beki and Aie River has been reflected. The events reflected in the short story like floods is a recurring event. We have seen that the Indigenous People are depended on their daily lives with the help of Indigenous Knowledge.

In the story, the lives of Khungkra and Nirmali has been reflected. We have seen the situation like floods which is a recurring event. The Bhutanese people have release water from the hills and the lives of the Indigenous People living near the Ujani Dongo river are facing lots of hardship due to floods. It has destroyed their property and livelihood.

The discussion between Khungkra and his wife Nirmali has been reflected as

The Bhutanese people are releasing water from the hills. The water may come like 7 to 8 feel tall at once and it may wash away everything by 2:30. Others have already packed up their belongings. Let's pack up our belongings like food and clothes. Iam going to make a canoe with our banana plant.

Some of the Indigenous food habits has been reflected from the words of Nirmali as follows

He has become more drunkard these days by becoming friends with the contractors. Today he will be attending someone's party for new car, tomorrow may be for someone's having son, day after tomorrow may be for someone's passing of final bill and so on.

3.1. Ujani Dongo

Ujani Dongo can be found in the short story Gongar Hajwni Dwi. Ujani Dongo is a river flowing near the house of Kungkra and Nirmali. When the Bhutanese people release the flood water from the hills, the river becomes overflooded and creates havoc every year. Kungkra's wife Nirmali has been narrating the incidents which occurs every year. The Indigenous People living near the river has to face the challenges of floods every year. The floods have been affecting their livelihood as well as livestock.

4.1. Challenges

Some of the challenges faced by the people living near the Ujani Dongo river are as follows :

1. To meet the challenges of floods, Khungkra has been preparing to make a canoe by cutting their big banana tree and bringing it in their courtyard and binding it up with bamboo right from 1 O'Clock in the night. His wife Nirmali has been packing up their belongings like clothes and food items.

5.1. Traditional curry

Some of the traditional curry reflected from the short story can be understood from the words of Nirmali like

"What curry are you going to get. Only snail and sour curry and dal and nothing else."

Snail, which can be found near the river is one of the traditional curry of the Indigenous People has been reflected in this story. Apart from that, the sour curry, which is a traditional curry of the Bodos are cultivated by themselves with the help of traditional knowledge has been reflected in this short story.

6.0. Conclusion

In this story, the river flowing from the Bhutan Hills and it's impacts on the lives of the Indigenous People has been reflected. In this story, the livelihood of the Indigenous People living in the plain areas and near the river has been reflected. Just like they are trying to be aware to meet the challenges of floods has been reflected. In this story, we have seen that Kungkra and his wife

Nirmali are trying to meet the challenges of floods by packing up their belongings like food and clothes as well as making a canoe to deal with the challenges of flood. In this story, the recurring incidents like floods and it's impacts like destruction of lives and property has been reflected. Some of the rivers like Aie, Beki (Bwrsi Dwima in Bodo language) and Ujani Dongo has also been reflected. But this is not a true story. May be it was an incident of the past. So it has been reflected in this story, but not history. We have seen the challenges faced by the Indigenous People from the story of Khungkra and Nirmali. The traditional curry of the Bodos has been reflected as well in this story. Snail, which can be found near the river is one of the traditional curry of the Indigenous People has been reflected in this story. Apart from that, the sour curry, which is a traditional curry of the Bodos are cultivated by themselves with the help of traditional knowledge has been reflected in this short story.

References

1. Basumatary, Z.D., Mr. Hybrid: Gwlwmdwi arw Mwdwi, Chirang Publication Board, Dhaligaon, Chirang (2005).
2. Basumatary, Rakhao, Boro Sungdo Soloni Jarimin (History of Bodo Short Stories) Words and Words, Bodoland, India (2013).
3. Chainary, Swarna Prabha, Boro Sungdo Soloni Bwhwiti Dahar (Edited), Saahitya Akademi, Bodo Department, Gauhati University, Second Edition (2014).
4. David Lodge & Nigel Wood (Edited), Modern Criticism and Theory, 2004 2nd Edition, Person Education (Singapore) pvt.Ltd. India Branch, 482 F.I.E. Patparagoni, Delhi 110092 India.
5. Waugh Patrica, Literary Theory and criticism, 2006, 1st Edition, OXFORD University Press, YMCA Library Building, Jaising Road New Delhi 11001.

www.ingramcontent.com/pod-product-compliance
Lightning Source LLC
LaVergne TN
LVHW021201160826
845679LV00024B/2206

9798891330290